The Coolest Guys 2

Featuring 35 of the top players from THE COOLEST GAME ON EARTH™

Text by Gary Mason & Barbara Gunn

Andrews McMeel
Publishing

Kansas City

THE COOLEST GUYS 2

98 99 00 01 02 TRC 10 9 8 7 6 5 4 3 2 1

Library of Congress Cataloging-in-Publication Data on file

Produced by Lionheart Books, Ltd.
Atlanta, Georgia 30341

Design: Jill Dible

Cover photos: Craig Melvin

TABLE OF CONTENTS

Introduction

NOW IT'S THEIR TURN.

With the retirement of the incomparable Wayne Gretzky, the torch has been passed to a new generation of National Hockey League superstars, a new legion of hockey players who have been handed the opportunity to take the game to an entirely new level.

Did Gretzky leave the game he loved so much in good hands? You bet. In some of the best.

Today, record numbers of hockey fans are being treated to some of the finest playmaking the game has seen. From the beauty of a Jaromir Jagr pass to the breathtaking speed of Pavel Bure. From the flare of Mike Modano to the brute force of Derian Hatcher.

These days, they come from all around the globe, these warriors of the National Hockey League. From Bromma, Sweden, to Kladno in the Czech Republic. From Moscow to Dryden, Ontario. And waiting in the wings are the

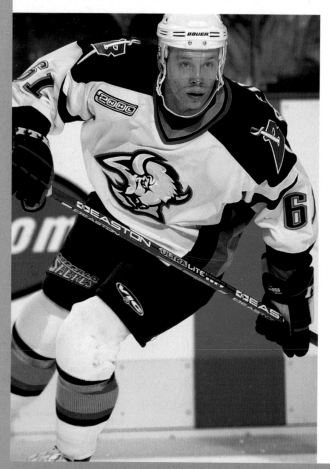

NHL's young guns, the rookies and sophomores who one day will have the torch passed to them. These are tomorrow's superstars. Players like Milan Hejduk of the Colorado Avalanche and Joe Thornton of the Boston Bruins. Curtis Brown of the Buffalo Sabres and Brad Stuart of the San Jose Sharks.

And there are players like Avalanche forward Chris Drury, who has traveled a star-blazed path to glory. Drury was the star pitcher for his Little League World Series champion Connecticut baseball team before he went on to win the Hobey Baker trophy as the best college hockey player in the U.S., which he added to his growing list of awards before winning the Calder Trophy as the NHL's top rookie.

Without question, he's a player who possesses an insatiable desire to win. "I guess it's just in my blood," Drury says in *Coolest Guys 2*. "It probably comes from being the youngest all my life. Just having to compete for every little thing at the dinner table or in football games in the backyard."

Impressing legions of fans, today's young guns are impressing veteran NHL teammates as well. Sabres forward Geoff Sanderson has often found himself standing slack-jawed watching the antics of rookie teammate Maxim Afinogenov.

"Max pulls a lot of tricks out of his bag," says Sanderson. "He's got the sweet hands and the sweet moves and he loves to dance. And he likes to beat guys more than once. He beats you once and he comes back and beats you again. It's great to watch."

And then there are the goalies, the fearless guardians of the net. There are tomorrow's greats, like the Sabres Martin Biron, and today's stars, like 1999-2000 Vezina-finalist Curtis Joseph of the Maple Leafs and Martin Brodeur of last season's Stanley Cup winning New Jersey Devils.

"I'm just having fun," says Brodeur, explaining why he is often found smiling behind his mask, no matter how tense the game. "I tend to look at the big picture rather than one game.

I tend not to get overwhelmed by one performance one way or the other."

The mark of a truly great sport is its ability to not only carry on but to thrive in the face of a loss as great as the retirement of Wayne Gretzky. But remember, Gretzky and the magnificent Mario Lemieux received the torch from the likes of Bobby Orr and Mike Bossy, who, in turn, were asked to take the game to new heights by the likes of Gordie Howe and Bobby Hull. This past year marked the passing of one of the game's most charismatic stars, Maurice "The Rocket" Richard. In death, Richard became a symbol of hockey's greatness and the greatness of those who play it, a symbol of that special player who was born to fly on ice, to lift a crowd to its feet, and put a smile on our faces.

As we stand at the dawn of a new millennium, we see the game of hockey as it has never been

played before. Certainly there's never been such speed and raw physical force. Never have the players been more skilled. And never have the young players entering the league better understood that it's their responsibility to respect and honour the accomplishments of those players who came before them, while setting their sights on new feats they have yet to achieve.

Joe Thornton, the Boston Bruins future superstar who, like many kids in Canada, grew up idolizing Wayne Gretzky, likes to tell the story of the night he went to Toronto Maple Leaf Gardens to watch his idol play for the first time. At the end of the second period, young Joe was in tears. His parents asked him what was wrong. A crying Joe explained the problem—Gretzky hadn't scored yet. But Gretzky wouldn't disappoint. He scored in the third period, and the future NHLer went home with a smile.

The Establishment

Rob Blake

WHEN ROB BLAKE TAKES TO THE ICE, he doesn't simply chase the puck—he also chases the opponent.

Most times, he'll make contact. And he'll usually leave someone sprawling, wondering what hit him.

Carolina's Andrei Kovalenko has fallen victim to the toughest hip-checker in the National Hockey League. So has Jochen Hecht of St. Louis and Sean Pronger of Boston. So, too, have countless others.

"He's a pretty big guy," says St. Louis defenseman Chris Pronger, "and when he gets you in his sight, you know you are going to get hit hard." "Hard" would be an understatement. When you're drilled by

Blake, the six four, 220 pound captain of the Los Angeles Kings, you're not simply checked. You're flattened.

"He tries to hit hard," says St. Louis coach Joel Quenneville. "He doesn't let up when it's time to make contact. Some guys hit to hurt, he's one of them."

That doesn't mean, however, that the Los Angeles blueliner is simply a one-man Demolition Derby. He also happens to be an exceptional skater who isn't half bad at scoring goals.

Last season, the thirty-year-old Blake, who's played his entire career for the Kings after being drafted by Los Angeles in 1988, not only tormented the opposition, he also scored 18 goals and 39 assists for an impressive 57 points.

In many ways, says ESPN hockey analyst Brian Engblom, Rob Blake represents the proverbial complete package.

"Blake's poke-checking ability, hitting, skating and shooting are exceptional," says Engblom. "What is underrated about Blake is his speed. He

"He swallows up ground quickly and just pounds people into the glass."

has huge strides, but they are quick. He can take two steps from the front of the net to the corner to hit somebody. He swallows up ground quickly and just pounds people into the glass."

Former coach Larry Robinson agrees that Blake pretty much has it all. "He gets from the front of the net to the corners as quick as anybody I've seen. And his shot! He has a great big shot. He's an all-around defenseman."

It was on the frozen ponds of his parents' farm, located in the small town of Simcoe, Ontario, that Blake first learned to play hockey. He was three years old.

At first, he wanted to play goal. Later on, as he began to grow—and tower above the other kids—Blake switched to defense. Hockey was always big, but so were other sports. Blake played soccer, baseball, basketball and volleyball, and didn't focus exclusively on hockey until after he had finished high school.

"I don't think it was until I went to college that I believed the NHL was a realistic dream," says Blake. "I was a kind of late developer." Late or not, Blake did develop—enormously. He enrolled at Bowling Green University in Ohio, where he played for the Falcons. He was twice named All-American, and in his junior year was a finalist for the Hobey Baker Award, given annually to the country's top college hockey player.

The wheels began to turn. L.A. began to focus on Blake, and in 1988 drafted him in the fourth round. In 1990, when Blake made his NHL debut, he began to really draw attention—in some cases from some pretty lofty circles.

"I don't know if he even knows how good he's going to be," observed then teammate Wayne Gretzky, when the twenty-year-old Blake first entered the big leagues.

In no time, Blake began to make an impact. In 1990–1991, he was named to the NHL All-Rookie team, and quickly established a reputation as a hard hitter who was also exceptional with the puck.

In 1993–1994, Blake established some personal bests—he scored 20 goals and added 48 assists for 68 points, and was named an NHL All-Star. But the following year, Blake's career took a nosedive: he would suffer the first of a series of injuries that would extend for three years and sideline him for 120 of 212 games.

"I thought I was invincible," recalls Blake, "and then you realize you're missing something you love to do, and that's playing hockey, and the only thing you want to do is get back."

Of course, Blake did get back, but not before some folks began questioning whether he had

what it took to be a star. He did. By 1997, Blake would be named best defenseman at the World Championships in Finland. In 1998, he would represent his country at the Winter Olympics in Nagano.

That same year Blake earned the big prize: he beat out Detroit's Nicklas Lidstrom and St. Louis's Chris Pronger to win the Norris Trophy as top defenseman in the NHL. The trophy shelf is heavy. But the ever ambititous Blake is still not completely satisfied. There's one last prize this tough guy would like to win before he hangs up the skates for good.

"Now the main thing is the Stanley Cup," he says. "I think that's what everyone ultimately plays for in this league."

#4 ROB BLAKE • Los Angeles Kings • Defense

			REGULAR SEASON					PLAYOFFS				
YEAR	TEAM	LEA	GP	G	A	TP	PIM	GP	G	A	TP	PIM
1987–88	Bowling Green	CCHA	43	5	8	13	88	.....	.....	.....	.....	.....
1988–89	Bowling Green	CCHA	46	11	21	32	140	.....	.....	.....	.....	.....
1989–90	Bowling Green	CCHA	42	23	36	59	140	.....	.....	.....	.....	.....
	Los Angeles	NHL	4	0	0	0	4	8	1	3	4	4
1990–91	Los Angeles	NHL	75	12	34	46	125	12	1	4	5	26
1991–92	Los Angeles	NHL	57	7	13	20	102	6	2	1	3	12
1992–93	Los Angeles	NHL	76	16	43	59	152	23	4	6	10	46
1993–94	Los Angeles	NHL	84	20	48	68	137			.....	.....	
1994–95	Los Angeles	NHL	24	4	7	11	38			.....	.....	
1995–96	Los Angeles	NHL	6	1	2	3	8			.....	.....	
1996–97	Los Angeles	NHL	62	8	23	31	82			.....	.....	
1997–98	Los Angeles	NHL	81	23	27	50	94	4	0	0	0	6
1998–99	Los Angeles	NHL	62	12	23	35	128	.....	.....	.....	.....	.....
1999–00	Los Angeles	NHL	77	18	39	57	112	4	0	2	2	4

Pavel Bure

IT WAS, WITHOUT QUESTION, ONE OF the finest compliments any hockey player could ever receive.

Last year, after Wayne Gretzky skated his last game with the National Hockey League and stepped off the ice and into retirement, he made a comment that created a minor sensation in the hockey world. He would have considered playing another year, he said, but only if the New York Rangers had managed to obtain a certain speedy winger.

That player was Pavel Bure.

"I think it's the biggest compliment I ever received or ever will receive in my life," says Bure. "I consider him the best player to ever play the game and there is nobody else who

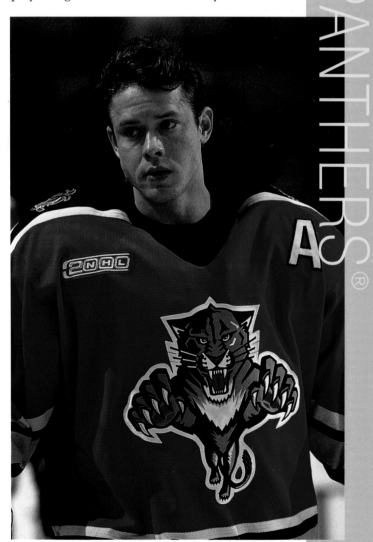

will ever get close."

As the history books will note, however, Gretzky's fantasy did not become a reality. Bure, who had played with the Vancouver Canucks for seven seasons and was looking for a change, would not become a Ranger but a Florida Panther instead.

And down there, in the land of sun and surf—and, yes, of chilly ice rinks—hockey hasn't been the same.

"Pavel is obviously our marquee guy," says Florida captain Scott Mellanby. It's a fact that's indisputable.

Last year, in his first complete season with Florida, Bure scored an impressive 58 goals and emerged as not only the top scorer in the Panther organization but in the entire National Hockey League. It would be enough to earn him the Rocket Richard Trophy, which is awarded annually to the top goal scorer in the NHL.

"There's no question about his skill level," says Tampa Bay goaltender Kevin Weekes. "He's hungry to score, he's hungry to shoot the puck, and he's hungry for breakaways."

In short, he's the kind of guy who terrorizes goaltenders and lifts hockey fans out of their seats. Watch the Russian Rocket and you get the

sense you're seeing someone with almost super-human speed skate down the ice.

He was only six when he first put on skates (dull figure skates, at that), but it took him no time to learn what to do with them. He progressed rapidly, propelled by a powerful work ethic. By the time he was sixteen, he was playing with the prestigious Red Army team.

Along the way, he would not only enter the record books, he would rewrite them. The native of Moscow, who remembers skipping school as a child to play pond hockey with younger brother Valeri, has won gold at the World Junior championships and the Olympic Games. After being drafted by Vancouver in 1989, he won the Calder Trophy as the NHL rookie of the year and twice posted 60 goal seasons.

In Florida, the twenty-nine-year-old has achieved the incredible and shattered multiple records. It was as a Panther that he posted his 500th NHL point on October 12, 1999, in a game against Montreal.

But while the stats books tell part of the story, they can't begin to describe the magic, the unbelievable electricity, that fires up an arena when Bure's on the ice. He is, many hockey fans agree, the most exciting player in the NHL today.

"He is a very electrifying player, brings a lot of fans out of their seats," says Valeri, who last year had an impressive season of his own, leading the Calgary Flames with 35 goals and 75 points. "I am his biggest fan and sometimes when I am watching, I am doing a lot of standing."

So, too, are a lot of other folks.

"He's electrifying," says New Jersey president Lou Lamoriello. "He's as exciting a hockey player as you'll find anywhere. You've got to be careful when you're playing against him that you don't stop and watch him. There's no question that with [Bure] the Panthers are one of the top teams in the league."

The folks who've been packing the National Car Rental Center all season have watched something amazing happen lately. With Bure on the ice, the Panthers have turned the ship around and raised their level of play.

"We were a boring team," says GM Bryan

Murray. "Now we're one of the most exciting."

Linemate Rob Niedermayer says Bure, who was last year named alternate captain by head coach Terry Murray, creates an almost palpable buzz whenever he takes to the ice. "It's sort of like just being in the building with Michael Jordan," he says. "There's just a special sort of feeling in the air."

Bure, says coach Murray, is the kind of hockey player who comes along once in a very rare while, the kind who can transform a team simply by wearing the uniform.

"He's the right guy for us to get behind," he says. "When a star of his calibre buys in, you become like an ocean liner. It gets going and it can't be stopped. The engine can even shut off, but the momentum you have keeps you moving for a long time."

#10 PAVEL BURE • Florida Panthers • Right Wing

			REGULAR SEASON					PLAYOFFS				
YEAR	TEAM	LEA	GP	G	A	TP	PIM	GP	G	A	TP	PIM
1987–88	CSKA	USSR	5	1	1	2	0	.....	.....	.....	.....	.....
1988–89	CSKA	USSR	32	17	9	26	8	.....	.....	.....	.....	.....
1989–90	CSKA	USSR	46	14	10	24	20	.....	.....	.....	.....	.....
1990–91	CSKA	USSR	44	35	11	46	24	.....	.....	.....	.....	.....
1991–92	Vancouver	NHL	65	34	26	60	30	13	6	4	10	14
1992–93	Vancouver	NHL	83	60	50	110	69	12	5	7	12	8
1993–94	Vancouver	NHL	76	60	47	107	86	24	16	15	31	40
1994–95	EV Landshut	Ger.	1	3	0	3	2	.....	.....	.....	.....	.....
	Spartak	CIS	1	2	0	2	2	.....	.....	.....	.....	.....
	Vancouver	NHL	44	20	23	43	47	11	7	6	13	10
1995–96	Vancouver	NHL	15	6	7	13	8	.....	.....	.....	.....	.....
1996–97	Vancouver	NHL	63	23	32	55	40	.....	.....	.....	.....	.....
1997–98	Vancouver	NHL	82	51	39	90	48	.....	.....	.....	.....	.....
	Russian Olympic		6	9	0	9	2	.....	.....	.....	.....	.....
1998–99	Florida	NHL	11	13	3	16	4	.....	.....	.....	.....	.....
1999–00	Florida	NHL	74	58	36	94	16	4	1	3	4	2

#33
Anson Carter

BY THE TIME ANSON CARTER WAS eight years old, he knew exactly what he wanted to do when he grew up. It wasn't a policeman or firefighter. It was an orthopedic surgeon.

By the time he was fourteen, the boy from Toronto had modified the goal a little. But he didn't abandon the medical dream, he simply added to it. He would, he decided, become both doctor *and* professional hockey player. And he would do it by securing a hockey scholarship to a top-rated U.S. college.

"We used to laugh at that so much," says Carter's mother, Valma. "But he's done two of the three things he said he would."

Indeed, he has. Carter did secure a scholarship to a first-rate American school—Michigan State. And he did end up as a professional

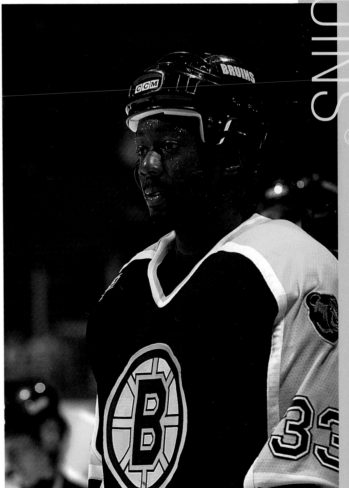

hockey player—as a star winger, in fact, for the Boston Bruins.

The only thing Carter did modify was the medical ambition; he entered Michigan State as a pre-med student but switched his major to sociology in his junior year when he decided to focus the bulk of his energy on sport. Anson Carter, it seems, has always been a goal-setter, even before he stepped on the ice.

His parents, who were teachers in Barbados before moving to Canada, describe their middle child as someone who was always determined, always headstrong, and always ahead of the pack. He was a straight A student right from the start, and at seven was invited to attend a school for gifted children. He didn't go, however, because he didn't want to leave his friends.

"So his teacher always had to find extra work for him," says Valma. "The regular work was never enough for him. It was that way all through public school."

Anson also knew, from the time he was a little boy, that hockey figured hugely in the career

"My parents were originally from Barbados," he says, "so the only ice they were used to seeing was in their drinking glasses."

plan. He'd played a lot of ball hockey and street hockey and aspired, more than anything, to play the game on ice.

There was one obstacle though—his parents.

Valma and husband Horace weren't crazy about the sport, which they considered too dangerous. In fact, says Anson, they knew little about it.

"My parents were originally from Barbados," he says, "so the only ice they were used to seeing was in their drinking glasses."

Carter, however, was not one to walk away quietly. He pushed and he pushed a little more and eventually his parents gave him permission to join a local youth league. Horace went further than that: he even followed the lead of the neighbors and flooded the backyard to make a rink.

Then, in spite of the fact that Carter could barely skate, things began to happen. Brian Ballantine, a Seattle Mariners scout and former major-junior goalie, ended up being Carter's first hockey coach, and was instantly impressed with Carter's size, attitude, work ethic and his intelligence.

"If he did it in practice," says Ballantine, "he'd do it again later in the season." Those who observed him back then say he progressed at an amazing rate. At the age of ten, he was named MVP of an international tournament in Boston. Two years later, says his linemate Adrian Sciarra, "it was obvious he was going to go a lot further than we were."

And go places, he did.

Carter persevered, ignoring the chides of some folks who told him that "black players don't make it to the NHL." "I would never listen to them," he says. "I was always focused and I knew what I had to do. I made a lot of sacrifices, like missing movie nights with my friends. And I had to get up early and train to make myself a better hockey player, so that when I did get the chance I wouldn't blow it." In 1992, Carter got the break he'd been waiting for: he was picked up by Quebec in the NHL Entry Draft. Carter, however, was busy playing for Michigan State, where he scored 102 goals and 68 assists for 170 points in 154 games.

Carter, who in 1994–95 was named as a finalist

for the Hobey Baker Award, given annually to the top college player in the U.S., was traded to Washington by Colorado in 1996 and then to Boston a year later.

Today, the twenty-six-year-old, six one Bruin is being hailed as one of the fastest, strongest, and most tenacious players in the National Hockey League. This past season, he scored 22 goals and added 25 assists in 59 games, proving the pundits right.

"He's got the whole package," says former Bruins defenseman Ray Bourque. "Speed, strength, moves and vision. He can be scary. And because he lives right and prepares himself, he's going to get better."

Carter, it seems, proves that some dreams, doggedly pursued, have a good chance of coming true.

"I just did what I thought was best," he says. "I've always been stubborn that way."

#33 ANSON CARTER • Boston Bruins • Right Wing

| YEAR | TEAM | LEA | REGULAR SEASON | | | | | PLAYOFFS | | | | |
			GP	G	A	TP	PIM	GP	G	A	TP	PIM
1992–93	Michigan State	CCHA	34	15	7	22	20	.....	.....	.....	.....	.....
1993–94	Michigan State	CCHA	39	30	24	55	36	.....	.....	.....	.....	.....
1994–95	Michigan State	CCHA	39	34	17	51	40	.....	.....	.....	.....	.....
1995–96	Michigan State	CCHA	42	23	20	43	36	.....	.....	.....	.....	.....
1996–97	Washington	NHL	19	3	2	5	7	.....	.....	.....	.....	.....
	Portland	AHL	27	19	19	38	11	.....	.....	.....	.....	.....
	Boston	NHL	19	8	5	13	2	.....	.....	.....	.....	.....
1997–98	Boston	NHL	78	16	27	43	31	6	1	1	2	0
1998–99	Utah	IHL	5	1	1	2	0	.....	.....	.....	.....	.....
	Boston	NHL	55	24	16	40	22	12	4	3	7	0
1999–00	Boston	NHL	59	22	25	47	14	.....	.....	.....	.....	.....

AS ONE OF THE MOST FEARED PLAYERS in the National Hockey League, Dallas Stars captain Derian Hatcher has never been one to shy away from physical contact.

And at six five and 230 pounds, they don't come in a much bigger package than the rugged Stars defenseman. When Dallas coach Ken Hitchcock taps his gigantic blueliner on the shoulder during a game, Hatcher is just as likely to jump over the boards and bang with devastating force the first thing he sees moving—that is, as long as that player isn't a teammate or his brother.

Now, it's not that Derian wouldn't bump his older brother Kevin, a defenseman with the New York Rangers, if he had the chance. Just don't ask Derian to square off against his older sibling the way, say, the Primeau brothers,

Wayne and Keith, did a few years ago.

"When we're out there, of course, I think of him as my brother," says Derian. "But I'm not going to let him score. I would hit him, but I wouldn't try to hit him hard. I don't think either one of us could just crush the other. We may grab each other, but I don't think you'd see us drop the gloves. How could you do that to your brother? It would seem a little weird to me."

Separated by six years, the twenty-eight-year-old Derian grew up in the suburbs of Detroit watching his older brother move through the minor hockey system ahead of him, into junior, and, eventually, the NHL.

"At that point it seemed like a bigger age difference," remembers Derian. "Kevin was becoming a man and I was a kid watching cartoons."

Derian would follow the same successful path as Kevin. Eventually their paths intersected when the two ended up on the same NHL team, the Dallas Stars. Kevin had spent the previous ten years with the Washington Capitals. When

he moved to Dallas, the brothers called it a "dream."

The dream, however, didn't last long.

During Kevin's two years with the Stars the team struggled and so, at times, did both of the brothers. The fans soon got on the back of the older, more experienced, Kevin. It was not an easy time for young Derian, especially when he had to listen to criticism of his brother, who was accused of being a distraction to his younger brother and stunting his growth as a player.

"The way everything ended just felt wrong," Derian now says of the two seasons in the mid-90s when the brothers were together. "I don't regret those two years at all. But it wasn't fair the way Kevin was treated by some people. I mean, I'm accountable for my own actions. They should have been blaming me, not my brother."

After Kevin left for Pittsburgh, and then the New York Rangers, Derian set about building his own identity in the league. Whereas his older brother was known for his offensive prowess, Derian became the typical stay-at-home defenseman. And the owner of one of the most crushing body checks in the game.

In his own quiet way, Derian Hatcher became a leader. Enough of one that he was made captain.

"He doesn't have to say a lot," says Stars head coach Ken Hitchcock. "His actions are very loud."

Hitchcock has come to rely on Hatcher defensively, the way he looks to forwards like Mike Modano and Brett Hull for their offensive touch. It is not uncommon for Hatcher to log more than thirty minutes a game, something he doesn't mind at all.

"I love the ice time," says Hatcher, who finished last season with 2 goals and 22 assists.

His opponents, on the other hand, would prefer to see less of him.

The highlight of Hatcher's nine-year NHL career came two seasons ago when the Stars marched to the Stanley Cup Finals against Dominik Hasek and the Buffalo Sabres. Hatcher was a dominating force on the Stars blueline throughout the final series, which ended in the early morning hours of Game 6. Brett Hull's goal in triple overtime put Hatcher, the team's captain, front and center.

"It was the most amazing feeling," recalls Hatcher when he held the Stanley Cup aloft. "It's a feeling I'll never forget for the rest of my life." Hatcher dreamed of holding the same Cup last season when the Stars made it to the finals again, this time against the New Jersey Devils. Again, Hatcher was a force throughout the series, especially in the final game, when he delivered a punishing body check on Devils' forward Petr Sykora that knocked the star New Jersey forward out of the game.

However, this Game 6 of the finals wouldn't have the same happy ending as the Game 6 of a year earlier. Like the one in 1998–99, it, too, went to overtime; but this time it was the Devils who scored the winner.

"It's disappointing," Hatcher says of the loss. "But we'll be back."

The Stars certainly will, if he has anything to do with it.

#2 DERIAN HATCHER • Dallas Stars • Defense

			REGULAR SEASON					PLAYOFFS				
YEAR	TEAM	LEA	GP	G	A	TP	PIM	GP	G	A	TP	PIM
1989–90	North Bay	OHL	64	14	38	52	81	5	2	3	5	8
1990–91	North Bay	OHL	64	13	49	62	163	10	2	10	12	28
1991–92	Minnesota	NHL	43	8	4	12	88	5	0	2	2	8
1992–93	Minnesota	NHL	67	4	15	19	178	.....	.....	.....	.....	.....
	Kalamazoo	IHL	2	1	2	3	21	.....	.....	.....	.....	.....
1993–94	Dallas	NHL	83	12	19	31	211	9	0	2	2	14
1994–95	Dallas	NHL	43	5	11	16	105	.....	.....	.....	.....	.....
1995–96	Dallas	NHL	79	8	23	31	129	.....	.....	.....	.....	.....
1996–97	Dallas	NHL	63	3	19	22	97	7	0	2	2	20
1997–98	Dallas	NHL	70	6	25	31	132	17	3	3	6	39
	US Olympic Team		4	0	0	0	0	.....	.....	.....	.....	.....
1998–99	Dallas	NHL	80	9	21	30	102	18	1	6	7	24
1999–00	Dallas	NHL	57	2	22	24	68	23	1	3	4	29

LONG BEFORE HE AMAZED FANS WITH his goal-scoring wizardry, Jaromir Jagr dreamt about freedom.

Like millions of Czech youngsters, Jagr grew up under the dictatorship of the Soviet Union. Even though he was born four years after the Prague Spring, the 1968 uprising by Czech citizens that was brutally quashed by Soviet armed forces, Jagr would have that year etched in his memory, for his resentment of the Russians had a deep history.

His grandparents were wealthy landowners when the Soviet army entered Prague in 1945, at the end of World War II, and took control from the provisional government that had been established. A few years later, Czechoslovakia was a communist country and Jagr's grandparents were poor.

"When the Communists came, they took it

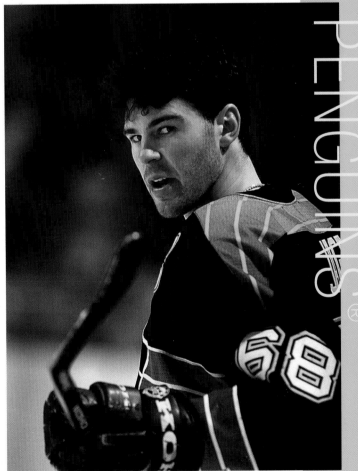

all," Jagr recalled. "So much land. So much land."

Jagr's grandfather, whom Jaromir speaks of affectionately though they never met, died in 1968 between the start of the Czech uprising and its tragic conclusion.

"At least my grandfather died in freedom," says Jagr proudly.

As a young boy, Jagr would go to school carrying a picture of America's president Reagan in his wallet. He dreamed of the day when he would move to the United States and experience real freedom. Of course, he made that journey to America and became one of the greatest stars of the National Hockey League. When he joined the Pittsburgh Penguins he took No. 68, a personal tribute to the Czech people's fight for freedom.

Jagr is coming off another brilliant season for the Pittsburgh Penguins and the team's new owner, Mario Lemieux. The fact that Jagr was now being paid by a former teammate took a little getting used to.

"It was strange," Jagr said of seeing Lemieux at practices in his capacity as owner, not player.

Jagr finished the 1999–2000 season with 96

points—tops in the league. He scored 42 goals and added 54 assists. What is even more amazing is that he compiled those numbers in only 63 games, as injuries kept him out of the lineup.

A finalist for the Hart Trophy as the league's most valuable player, Jagr lost to St. Louis Blues' defenseman Chris Pronger. Pronger edged out Jagr by one vote—396 to 395—the closest balloting in the award's seventy-six-year history.

Jagr would not go home empty handed, however. He won the Art Ross Trophy as the league's top scorer for the fourth consecutive season. As well, he received the Lester B. Pearson Award, which is given to the league MVP as voted on by the players.

"I've said before this means so much to me because it is voted on by the players," said Jagr.

There are no signs Jagr plans to slow the torrid scoring pace he's set since he entered the league, though he remains typically modest about his achievements.

"For me," says Jagr, "the game is just a fun game. Being the MVP is not my goal. I just want to show some moves, have some fun. That's what it's about."

Coaches and players, past and present, rave about his abilities.

"Jaromir is as close to the best player as there is, if not the best," says Kevin

Constantine, former coach of the Penguins. "There are certain things I think Jaromir does better than anyone, such as protecting the puck and playing one-on-one."

Hockey legend Wayne Gretzky agrees.

"He's smart, he's a good skater, and, most important in my opinion, he has great size and knows how to use it," says Gretzky. "He's the kind of guy who only comes along once in awhile."

Jagr has been a colourful addition to the league. Once recognized by the long, flowing locks that spilled out from the back of his helmet, Jagr arrived this season with his curly black hair cut short. He added dash by saluting to the crowd following a goal before ditching that move in favour of blowing a kiss to his fans.

"It's just fun stuff," says the twenty-eight-year-old forward. While the Penguins two Stanley Cup victories in the early 1990s must certainly rank high on Jagr's list of accomplishments, it's probably a safe bet that his crowning achievement as a hockey player came in 1998 when he and his teammates from the Czech Republic defied the odds and won gold at the Nagano Olympics. Particularly sweet for Jagr, perhaps, was the fact the gold medal victory came against the Russians.

"It's a different people now," says Jagr. "It's

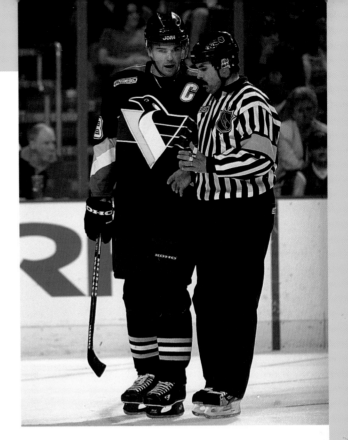

not their fault. But I'm glad we beat their team."

After the gold medal game, Jagr and his teammates returned to Prague where 100,000 of their fellow countrymen jammed into Wenceslas Square to cheer their great victory. Jagr was greeted by one of the greatest rounds of applause.

Somewhere high above the scene, you had to believe, a grandfather was smiling.

#68 JAROMIR JAGR • Pittsburgh Penguins • Right Wing

| YEAR | TEAM | LEA | REGULAR SEASON | | | | | PLAYOFFS | | | | |
			GP	G	A	TP	PIM	GP	G	A	TP	PIM
1988–89	Kladno	Czech.	39	8	10	18	4	.....	.....	.....	.....	.....
1989–90	Kladno	Czech.	51	30	29	59	.....	.....	.....	.....	.....	.....
1990–91	Pittsburgh	NHL	80	27	30	57	42	24	3	10	13	6
1991–92	Pittsburgh	NHL	70	32	37	69	34	21	11	13	24	6
1992–93	Pittsburgh	NHL	81	34	60	94	61	12	5	4	9	23
1993–94	Pittsburgh	NHL	80	32	67	99	61	6	2	4	6	16
1994–95	Kladno	Czech.	11	8	14	22	10	.....	.....	.....	.....	.....
	Bolzano	Euro.	5	8	8	16	4	.....	.....	.....	.....	.....
	Bolzano	Italy	1	0	0	0	0	.....	.....	.....	.....	.....
	Schalke	Ger. 2	1	1	10	11	0	.....	.....	.....	.....	.....
	Pittsburgh	NHL	48	32	38	70	37	12	10	5	15	6
1995–96	Pittsburgh	NHL	82	62	87	149	96	18	11	12	23	18
1996–97	Pittsburgh	NHL	63	47	48	95	40	5	4	4	8	4
1997–98	Pittsburgh	NHL	77	35	67	102	64	6	4	5	9	2
	Czech Olympic		6	1	4	5	2	.....	.....	.....	.....	.....
1998–99	Pittsburgh	NHL	81	44	83	127	66	9	5	7	12	16
1999–00	Pittsburgh	NHL	63	42	54	96	50	11	8	8	16	6

PAUL KARIYA HAS ALWAYS BEEN A reader, but not when it came to the newspaper. He devoured novels, but seldom the sports section.

Last season, all that changed. Kariya, the gifted captain of the Anaheim Mighty Ducks, started scanning the papers like he never had before—not because he was looking for his own name but because he was looking for mention of someone else.

That other, younger Kariya.

"I won't read a word about myself," says Paul, "but I can't get enough about him."

The "him," of course, is Steve Kariya, Paul's kid brother. The North Vancouver twenty-three-year-old made his National Hockey League debut by hitting the ice with the Vancouver Canucks.

It was, of course, a media event. Hockey

MIGHTY DUCKS OF ANAHEIM®

fans everywhere were devouring every detail about Steve's entry into the NHL—and no one more than Paul.

"Paul never reads a word about himself, but there he is wanting a play-by-play on every word anyone wrote about Steve," says Michiko Kariya, eldest of the Kariya siblings. Paul, she says, would routinely ask her to plug into the Internet, find stories about Steve, and send them off to him in California. "He kept asking, 'What is the media saying about Steve?'"

As it happens, they were saying the nicest things. They were pointing out that Steve was fast, like Paul. And focused too. He was dedicated and determined, and, like Paul, he was a graduate of the University of Maine where he played for the Black Bears.

The media spotlight may have been a new

experience for Steve—and in some ways, maybe even an unsettling one—but Paul has had to deal with it for a long time. In his case, the hype was established even before the day in 1993 when he was picked up by the Mighty Ducks in the first round of the NHL Entry Draft.

Perhaps it was in 1991–92 that the attention began in earnest—the season Kariya accumulated 132 points in forty junior games in Penticton, British Columbia. Perhaps it was the next season, when he scored 25 goals and added 75 assists in just 39 college games at Maine and became the first freshman to win the Hobey Baker Award, hockey's version of the Heisman Trophy.

Perhaps it was in 1994 that the Kariya name became even better known—that was the year he helped lead Team Canada to a silver medal in the Winter Olympics. Then again, perhaps it was later on, after the left winger entered the NHL and immediately began to establish himself as a player whose speed was as rare as his

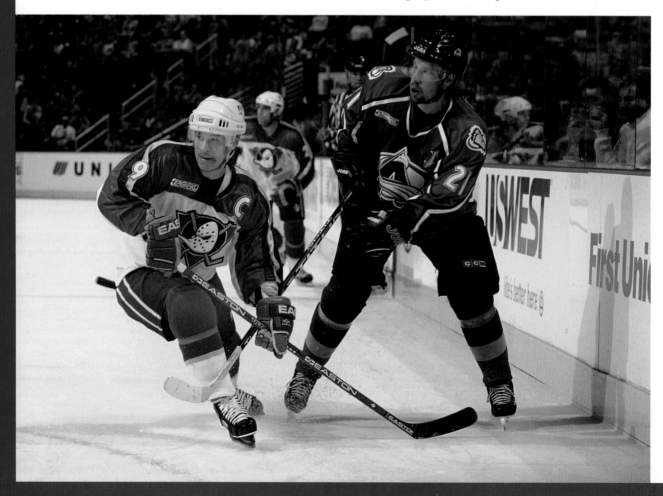

work ethic. From that point on, the media knew—as did the fans—that Kariya was not the kind of hockey player to come along every day. He was wily, he was powerful, and he was possessed of that brand of gentlemanly conduct that would twice win him hockey's greatest sportsmanship award, the Lady Byng.

"Paul Kariya is the most focused, most intense athlete I have ever been around," says Duck coach Craig Hartsburg. "It's refreshing, I think, for a professional athlete and superstar to be like that. He approaches the game with a passion that he loves."

Kariya, who has been identified by some in the NHL as the ideal person to assume Wayne Gretzky's role as hockey's ambassador, possesses something that Hartsburg doesn't see every day: the drive to raise himself to even greater heights of achievement.

"The average player, if he's consistent, that's very good," says Hartsburg. "But great players . . . at times, there's another level in their game that they can go to that even good players just can't reach. Paul has done that lately."

He's matured on the ice—by season's end, he'd led the Ducks in total points with 86—but those who know Paul Kariya will say that he's also matured as a person.

The twenty-six-year-old, who is invariably spoken of as a humble and intelligent man, was once so intensely private he would not eat in restaurants and avoided all contact with the media. These days, that's changed. Kariya may still be a private person, but he's more

comfortable with his public role.

"To me, the evolution of Paul Kariya has been a gradual willingness to embrace the other things in life," says Stu Grimson, who played with the Ducks during Kariya's rookie year.

"Whether it be the media, the fans, or other things outside the game, he slowly has learned and been more willing to accommodate these things, knowing he doesn't have to sacrifice part of his game preparation for them." Indeed, Paul Kariya has sacrificed nothing. He is still the kind of person any brother would want to emulate, the kind who believes that hockey, however important, ranks second to something else.

"You'd love to have won the Stanley Cup," he says. "[But] I'd like to be remembered mostly as a good person."

#9 PAUL KARIYA • Mighty Ducks of Anaheim • Left Wing

			REGULAR SEASON					PLAYOFFS				
YEAR	TEAM	LEA	GP	G	A	TP	PIM	GP	G	A	TP	PIM
1992–93	U. of Maine	H.E.	39	25	75	100	12	.....	.....	.....	.....	.....
1993–94	U. of Maine	H.E.	12	8	16	24	4	.....	.....	.....	.....	.....
	Cdn. National	.....	23	7	34	41	2	.....	.....	.....	.....	.....
	Cdn. Olympic	.....	8	3	4	7	2	.....	.....	.....	.....	.....
1994–95	Anaheim	NHL	47	18	21	39	4	.....	.....	.....	.....	.....
1995–96	Anaheim	NHL	82	50	58	108	20	.....	.....	.....	.....	.....
1996–97	Anaheim	NHL	69	44	55	99	6	11	7	6	13	4
1997–98	Anaheim	NHL	22	17	14	31	23	.....	.....	.....	.....	.....
1998–99	Anaheim	NHL	82	39	62	101	40	3	1	3	4	0
1999–00	Anaheim	NHL	74	42	44	86	24	.....	.....	.....	.....	.....

IT WAS NOT A ROLE JOHN LECLAIR had wanted to play, but for a few days during last season's Stanley Cup playoffs the Philadelphia Flyers' bruising left winger became the poster boy for what the NHL's post-season has become—a battle.

During Game 3 of the Eastern Conference finals between Philadelphia and New Jersey, LeClair went for the puck behind the Devils' net. So did New Jersey goalie Martin Brodeur, who got to it first and attempted to clear it out of his end. The follow-through of Brodeur's stick caught LeClair in the face, opening a nasty cut along his nose toward his eye. The wound took thirty-six stitches to close.

If it had been the regular season, LeClair probably would have missed several games recuperating, but this was the playoffs and

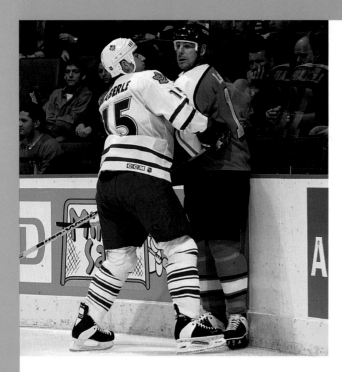

LeClair's rise to stardom in the NHL had humble beginnings. He started his career with the storied Montreal Canadiens. There LeClair was a steady, third-line left winger whose primary job was to stop the other team's best players from scoring. While wearing the Habs' famous red, white and blue, LeClair had a couple of 19-goal seasons he seemed quite content with.

However, the highlight of his career with Montreal occurred during the 1992–1993 season, when the Canadiens made an improbable march to the Stanley Cup Finals. In Games 3 and 4 of the finals against the Los Angeles Kings, LeClair scored crucial overtime winners.

Jacques Demers, the Canadiens coach at the time, would later say: "All I know is that I have a Stanley Cup ring I owe to John LeClair."

When LeClair was traded to Philadelphia in February 1995, his career changed forever. Bobby Clarke's plan was to put LeClair alongside the Flyers resident superstar, Eric Lindros.

LeClair was elated.

In the remaining 37 games of the 1995 season, LeClair scored 25 goals. It was, as they say, the beginning of a beautiful friendship. For the next five seasons, LeClair would often park himself in front of his opponent's net, deflecting in shots from the point or getting rebounds from teammates and putting the puck behind the goaltender. For the first few seasons with the Flyers, LeClair would be paired with Lindros and Mikael Renberg, forming the famous line known as the Legion of Doom. For John LeClair, it was like hitting the jackpot. Between 1995 and 1998, LeClair would have 51-, 50-, and 51-goal seasons.

"Never in my wildest dreams did I think I'd become a 50-goal scorer," says LeClair. "If you look back on it, it's not like I played great hockey every single night. A lot of those 50-goal [seasons] have to be attributed to my teammates."

Last season LeClair scored 40 goals and added 37 assists. While he continued to establish himself as one of the best power forwards in the game, LeClair also reinforced his reputation as one of the game's great humanitarians.

Early in his career, LeClair established a foundation in his name to benefit needy children

LeClair was one of the Flyers' most important warriors. With every game a crucial battle, LeClair decided to attach a visor to his helmet and go to war.

"It's a playoff game and people are going to play hard," LeClair said at the time. "So, I'm not going to worry about it. I'll play the way I always play."

For several days, LeClair's mangled mug became one of the most photographed faces in the world. The dark stitches that ran like a jagged road along his nose, the bruise under his eye, and even more stitches that were put in just over his eyelid became a symbol of what playoff hockey is all about. The fact that the six foot three, 230 pound behemoth from St. Albans, Vermont, became synonymous with the kind of grit and determination necessary to play the game of hockey was appropriate, for in a stellar ten-year NHL career LeClair has established himself as one of the game's most intense and fiery competitors.

"John is a great player," says Flyers GM Bob Clarke. "He gives you everything he has every shift, every night."

"Never in my wildest dreams did I think I'd become a 50-goal scorer," says LeClair.

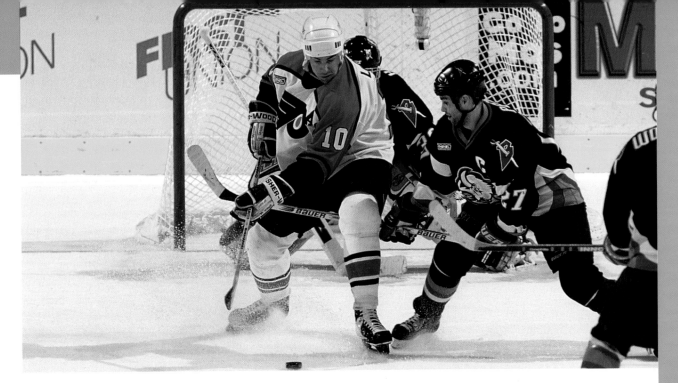

and youth groups in Vermont. The foundation initially set a modest goal of $5,000, but in its first four years it distributed more than $100,000 to numerous groups, including Camp Ta-Kum-Ta, a summer getaway for children with cancer. Not far from his home in St. Albans, Camp Ta-Kum-Ta was one of the first places LeClair took the Stanley Cup when, as tradition dictates, he was allowed to keep it for a few days following the Habs' win in 1993.

"I just think it's a satisfying opportunity to show appreciation for the support of the whole state," says LeClair. "Through the foun-dation I can give something back."

Last season, LeClair continued to prove he was more than just a great hockey player. He and wife Christina launched the John LeClair Face-Off Against Hunger campaign, an initiative to help hungry families in the Philadelphia area. When his NHL career wraps up, John LeClair will be remembered as one of the game's most feared players and most prolific goal scorers. But, perhaps more importantly, John LeClair will be remembered for a kind heart.

Which should be worth a Hall of Fame all its own.

#10 JOHN LECLAIR • Philadelphia Flyers • Left Wing

			REGULAR SEASON					PLAYOFFS				
YEAR	TEAM	LEA	GP	G	A	TP	PIM	GP	G	A	TP	PIM
1987–88	U. of Vermont	ECAC	31	12	22	34	62	.....	.....	.....	.....	.....
1988–89	U. of Vermont	ECAC	18	9	12	21	40	.....	.....	.....	.....	.....
1989–90	U. of Vermont	ECAC	10	10	6	16	38	.....	.....	.....	.....	.....
1990–91	U. of Vermont	ECAC	33	25	20	45	58	.....	.....	.....	.....	.....
	Montreal	NHL	10	2	5	7	2	3	0	0	0	0
1991–92	Montreal	NHL	59	8	11	19	14	8	1	1	2	4
	Fredericton	AHL	8	7	7	14	10	2	0	0	0	4
1992–93	Montreal	NHL	72	19	25	44	33	20	4	6	10	14
1993–94	Montreal	NHL	74	19	24	43	32	7	2	1	3	8
1994–95	Montreal	NHL	9	1	4	5	10	.....	.....	.....	.....	.....
	Philadelphia	NHL	37	25	24	49	20	15	5	7	12	4
1995–96	Philadelphia	NHL	82	51	46	97	64	11	6	5	11	6
1996–97	Philadelphia	NHL	82	50	47	97	58	19	9	12	21	10
1997–98	Philadelphia	NHL	82	51	36	87	32	5	1	1	2	8
1998–99	Philadelphia	NHL	76	43	47	90	30	6	3	0	3	12
1999–00	Philadephia	NHL	82	40	37	77	36	18	6	7	13	6

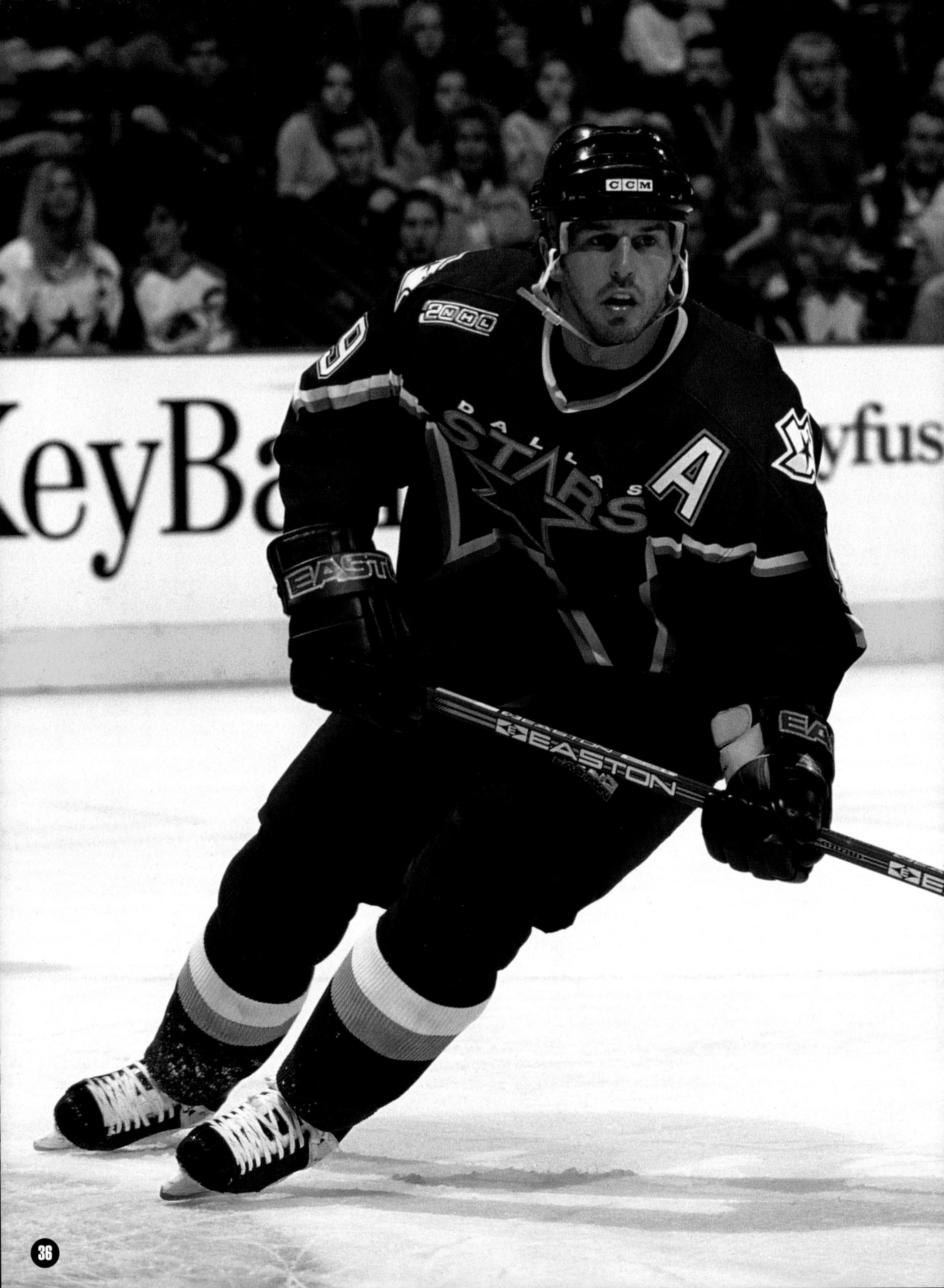
CCM
DALLAS
STARS
A
EASTON

THERE ARE MANY NATIONAL HOCKEY League players who can fly at supersonic speeds, but what separates the superstars from the rest of the pack is the ability to carry the puck while they're doing it. Take, for example, Dallas Stars center Mike Modano.

"What he's able to do with the puck at a high speed might be the most amazing part of Mike's game," says Stars captain Derian Hatcher. "I've played with him for nine years and this is the best I've ever seen him."

Yes, the 1999–2000 season was another special one for Modano. His 81 points—38 goals and 43 assists—led the team. And when Hatcher was out of action for nine weeks with an injury, it was Modano who wore the

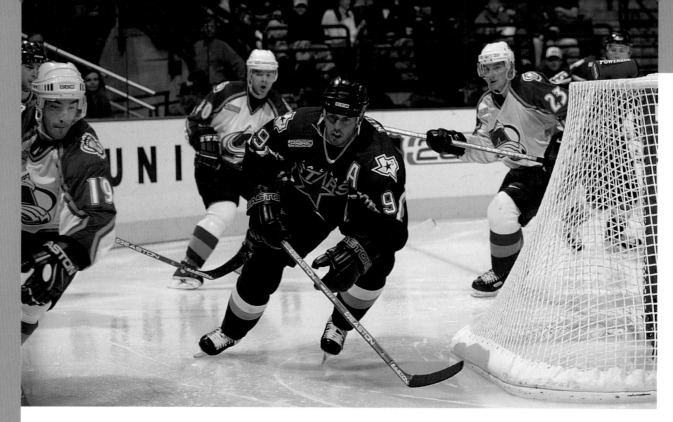

captain's insignia and led the Stars into battle each night.

But it was another spectacular season that almost never came to pass. On October 2, in a game against the Anaheim Mighty Ducks, Modano was checked from behind by Ducks defenseman Ruslan Salei, sending Modano head-first into the boards, his head twisting grotesquely as it crunched against the base. For days afterward, television replayed this sickening sight on sports programs and the nightly news.

Modano, who was lucky not to have broken his neck, suffered sprained neck ligaments, a mild concussion, and a broken nose. Amazingly, he would miss only three games. Salei would be suspended for ten games for the hit. The incident frightened Modano, and in the days that followed he spoke out against unnecesary violence. Not only was Mike Modano a superstar player, he was quickly becoming the conscience of the game.

Despite his injuries, Modano refused to change his style of play, which has electrified crowds in NHL cities for eleven seasons now.

"He's one of the best two-way players in the world," says his coach, Ken Hitchcock. "He's a threat from anywhere on the ice."

Brendan Morrow, the Stars fine rookie winger, had the good fortune of playing with Modano for most of last season.

"Mike plays well when he pulls the goaltender and both defensemen toward him," says Morrow. "And all I have to do is stand in front of a wide open net with my stick on the ice."

Wayne Gretzky, who played against Modano in many hard-fought games, says the thirty-year-old Michigan native is one of the elite players in the game.

"If you can play the game at this level, at that speed, and see the ice, well, that's special," says Gretzky. "He's the kind of player the game needs."

Modano and Hitchcock have had their ups and downs over the years but both have enormous respect for one another. It is quite common for Hitchcock to phone Modano at home on the eve of a big game and ask him point blank what he is going to bring to the game the next day.

If it's every NHL player's dream to win the Stanley Cup, Modano's dream came true two seasons ago. And the flashy center was a big reason why. Modano was outstanding throughout the 1998–99 playoffs, but never more so than during the final series against Buffalo. Playing with a broken wrist, Modano not only crashed opponents and shot the puck, but also won important faceoffs.

"It was a really gutsy performance," remembers Hitchcock. "Mike Modano really showed what he was made of."

Over the years, Modano's game has changed. Once known mostly for his beautiful skating abilities and a terrific goal-scoring touch—he scored 50 goals the first year the Minnesota franchise moved to Dallas in 1993–94—Modano has become equally known for his defensive abilities. Hitchcock will routinely put Modano out against the other team's top-scoring line. He may not win a scoring title before his career is finished, but he says he'll take a Stanley Cup over a scoring title any day.

"When you see a player with his skill dig in as hard as he does on defense, it shows how much he cares about the team, says Stars assistant coach Doug Jarvis. "That's a consummate team player."

Meanwhile, Modano is making sure he'll be set for a life after hockey. He has invested earnings from his recent $43.5 million contract wisely. Last year, he became involved in a deal with three highly successful technology firms in Dallas to build an incubator company that provides financial and marketing assistance to develop Internet firms under one umbrella. He's also involved in developing the official Web site for NHL players.

Last year's march to the Stanley Cup Final ended in disappointment for the Dallas Stars. But Modano remained a force throughout the final, and looks to be a player with many good years ahead of him.

"He is a player committed more to winning than stats, more to substance than style," says coach Ken Hitchcock. "And he has a ring on his finger because of it."

#9 MIKE MODANO • Dallas Stars • Center

			REGULAR SEASON					PLAYOFFS				
YEAR	TEAM	LEA	GP	G	A	TP	PIM	GP	G	A	TP	PIM
1986–87	Prince Albert	WHL	70	32	30	62	96	8	1	4	5	4
1987–88	Prince Albert	WHL	65	47	80	127	80	9	7	11	18	18
1988–89	Prince Albert	WHL	41	39	66	105	74	.....	.....	.....	.....	.....
	Minnesota	NHL	.....	.....	.....	.....	.....	2	0	0	0	0
1989–90	Minnesota	NHL	80	29	46	75	63	7	1	1	2	12
1990–91	Minnesota	NHL	79	28	36	64	65	23	8	12	20	16
1991–92	Minnesota	NHL	76	33	44	77	46	7	3	2	5	4
1992–93	Minnesota	NHL	82	33	60	93	83	.....	.....	.....	.....	.....
1993–94	Dallas	NHL	76	50	43	93	54	9	7	3	10	16
1994–95	Dallas	NHL	30	12	17	29	8	.....	.....	.....	.....	.....
1995–96	Dallas	NHL	78	36	45	81	63	.....	.....	.....	.....	.....
1996–97	Dallas	NHL	80	35	48	83	42	7	4	1	5	0
1997–98	Dallas	NHL	52	21	38	59	32	17	4	10	14	12
	US Olympic Team		4	2	0	2	0	.....	.....	.....	.....	.....
1998–99	Dallas	NHL	77	34	47	81	44	23	5	18	23	16
1999–00	Dallas	NHL	77	38	43	81	48	23	10	13	23	10

Owen Nolan

MOST GUYS WHO END UP IN THE National Hockey League have one thing in common: they've been playing the game for as long as they can remember. Not so with Owen Nolan. His contemporaries may have spent most of their formative years on frozen ponds, but that wasn't the case with him. He didn't even put on a pair of ice skates until he was nine years old. And even then it was only because the skates—secondhand ones—were given to his family.

His parents, of course, were far from your typical hockey types. They hailed from Belfast, Northern Ireland, and knew considerably more about hurling—an Irish pastime that resembles lacrosse—than they did about that peculiar sport that involves ice, sticks, and a three-inch chunk of rubber.

SAN JOSE SHARKS™

"But they raised me well, to be a good person," recalls Nolan, who emigrated with his parents to Canada from Northern Ireland when he was just seven months old. "They encouraged me to be competitive, to have the desire to win."

Nolan had that desire—in spades. Growing up just outside Toronto, he discovered he had a passion for all things athletic. He played soccer and baseball, and when he laced up those skates he soon played something else—hockey.

"I didn't take it seriously at first," says Nolan, who remembers feeling like a bit of a latecomer when he first played the game. "I just went out and messed around."

But Nolan had no difficulty making up for lost time as he acquired the skills of his peers and then moved beyond them.

By the time he was eighteen, Nolan would not only feel completely comfortable in his skates, he would also be good enough to be considered the best junior anywhere—good enough to become the first player picked in the 1990 NHL Entry Draft, ahead of Jaromir Jagr, Keith Primeau, and Petr Nedved. The team was the Quebec Nordiques. They may not have been the strongest in the league, but the feisty right winger—now the much cherished captain of the San Jose Sharks—had a tremendous time anyway. "There were six or seven of us around the same age. We grew up together. We were all like brothers. We played together for five years. That was probably the best thing about being in Quebec, the friends I made. The worst thing was the weather. It was cold there!"

Nolan befriended numerous Nordiques—including Adam Foote, Mike Ricci, and Iain Fraser—and quickly established himself as a strong player with finely honed skills, tremendous hockey smarts, and an uncanny knack for scoring goals.

"I always thought Owen Nolan was a great player," says Flyers defenseman Luke Richardson. "He's a great power forward, tough as nails, and capable of playing thirty minutes each game."

Richardson isn't alone in his assessment of the guy they call "Buster," a player who's considered as tough—and, yes, as mean—as he is skilled. In 1992, just two years after he was drafted, Nolan was considered strong enough to attend the NHL All-Star Game. On two occasions since then, in 1996 and 1997, he's made the return trip.

"He can do it all," says fellow Shark Jeff Friesen, who plays left wing on Nolan's line. "He's the whole package of a power forward. And there's only a certain few power forwards in the game."

Nolan played briefly with Colorado—the Nordiques successors—before being traded to San Jose in a deal that saw Sandis Ozolinsh head the other way. The October 1995 trade would come as a blow to Nolan, since Colorado was a Stanley Cup contender, and the Sharks, as a junior team, were far weaker. It would be even more painful for Nolan when the Avs would go on to win the Cup that year.

"Everyone's goal in this league is to win the Stanley Cup," he explains. "To be so close and then get pulled away like that, and then knowing you have to wait several years before you get another shot . . . it's frustrating."

Nonetheless, Nolan would continue to work hard in San Jose. In each year since Nolan was acquired, the Sharks' fortunes have improved. In the last two years, they've made the playoffs and become true contenders—thanks, in great measure, to their captain, who last season posted 44 goals and 40 assists for an amazing 84 points.

"It's great to come to the rink knowing you have a chance of winning every night," says Nolan. "In the past, we'd get beat up and lose and it was tough to come to the rink motivated every day. Now we have a great group of guys and we know we'll win the majority of our games." Linemate Friesen agrees that teamwork is all-important, but he also knows the difference a captain can make.

"Give him credit," says Friesen. "He stuck it out and he's become a great leader for us. He knows there's a lot of people that look up to him. "He's our captain and when he says something, you better listen, because he wants to win."

#11 OWEN NOLAN • San Jose Sharks • Right Wing

			REGULAR SEASON					PLAYOFFS				
YEAR	TEAM	LEA	GP	G	A	TP	PIM	GP	G	A	TP	PIM
1988–89	Cornwall	OHL	62	34	25	59	213	19	5	11	16	41
1989–90	Cornwall	OHL	58	51	59	110	240	6	7	5	12	26
1990–91	Halifax	AHL	6	4	4	8	11	.....	.....	.....	.....	.....
	Quebec	NHL	59	3	10	13	109	.....	.....	.....	.....	.....
1991–92	Quebec	NHL	75	42	31	73	183					
1992–93	Quebec	NHL	73	36	41	77	185	5	1	0	1	2
1993–94	Quebec	NHL	6	2	2	4	8	.....	.....	.....	.....	.....
1994–95	Quebec	NHL	46	30	19	49	46	6	2	3	5	3
1995–96	Colorado	NHL	9	4	4	8	9					
	San Jose	NHL	72	29	32	61	146	.....	.....	.....	.....	.....
1996–97	San Jose	NHL	72	31	32	63	155	.....	.....	.....	.....	.....
	Canada	World Ch.	10	4	3	7	31	.....	.....	.....	.....	.....
1997–98	San Jose	NHL	75	14	27	41	144	6	2	2	4	26
1998–99	San Jose	NHL	78	19	26	45	129	6	1	1	2	6
1999–00	San Jose	NHL	78	44	40	84	110	10	8	2	10	6

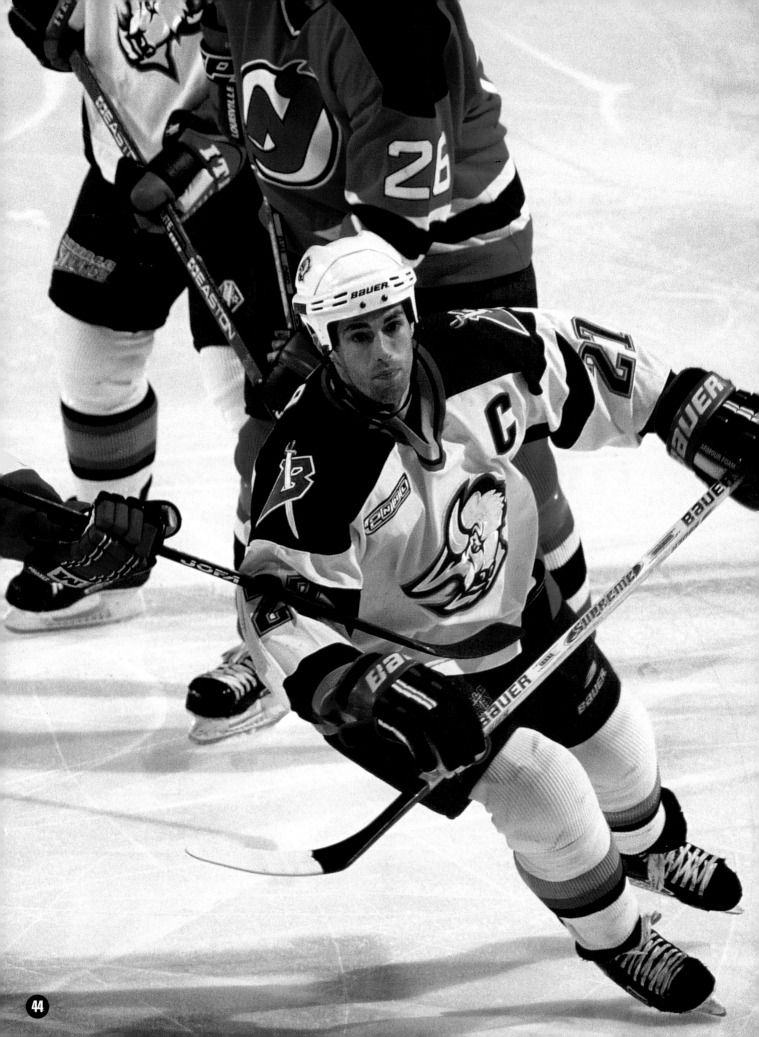

FOR AS LONG AS HE'S PLAYED HOCKEY, Michael Peca has been a hit. Literally. He may never have been one of the biggest guys on the team, but that never seemed to matter. He was tough regardless.

"Michael was a hitter from day one," says Peca's mom, Kim. "I was never afraid for him because I knew he could handle himself."

Anyone who's paid passing notice of the Buffalo Sabres captain knows that looks can be deceiving. Peca is small by National Hockey League standards—he's five ten and weighs 180 pounds—and appears innocent and unassuming. Off-ice, when he dons the wire-rimmed spectacles, you might associate Peca more with a classroom or a library than an ice rink. But Peca is anything but docile and no one knows that better than Teemu Selanne, Chris Simon, Steve Martins, Tie Domi or any of the other players Peca has

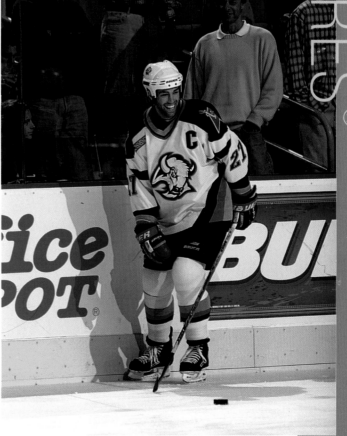

Wolves GM Sam McMaster back in 1990, when he made Peca his No.1 draft choice. "He'll definitely play in the NHL."

"Oh, yeah," a reporter replied. "How big is he?"

"Five seven, 150 pounds."

"Sam," the reporter commented. "He'll never play in the NHL."

But Peca, of course, would prove otherwise. After posting some pretty remarkable years as a junior—he showed himself to be an offensive specialist by posting 113 points in 55 games during one fairly typical year—he was drafted by the Vancouver Canucks.

After graduating from the junior ranks, Peca discovered that ice time was at a premium so he began to crank up the physical play and ended up demonstrating that he could make the biggest contribution as a defensive forward.

"I knew that it was an opportunity for me to take on this special role and establish myself," recalls Peca of the new job he had assumed. "I just wanted to make the best of it. I always felt that I've always been a solid two-way player."

It was in 1995 when Peca joined the Sabres after an off-season trade that he truly began to demonstrate his value.

"Our scouting staff was always very high on him," remembers Larry Carriere, Sabres assistant GM at the time. "He's what being a Buffalo Sabre is all about."

In no time, Peca began to be seen as the guy who could stop the opposition's big stars. He delivered some hits that would become legendary, but at the same time he proved he could still be an offensive threat. In 1996–97, the year he won the Selke, Peca ended the season with 20 goals and 29 assists for 49 points.

"I don't know if I've seen a guy who can go two ways the way he does, with the hitting and the offense and the defense all in one," says Sabre coach Lindy Ruff. "And I think he's the one guy who can change the direction of a hockey game with one hit and the other team knows that. A lot of them won't admit it, but they know he's out there."

Peca, who has become one of the most feared hitters in the National Hockey League, is routinely

smashed into since he was summoned to the big leagues back in 1992. Gentle he ain't.

"To me, it just seemed natural to hit," says the twenty-six-year-old Peca, looking back on his years in hockey, which began in the middle-class town of Brampton, Ontario.

"Every team had this guy who could prematurely grow a beard who everybody said was six three but was really five nine. I always targeted those guys. Then, when they tried to get me back, the biggest challenge was to stay on my feet."

Peca, who won the Selke Trophy as the NHL's best defensive forward in 1997 and was a close runner-up for the prize in 1998 and 1999, became an item of conversation in Ontario Hockey League circles years ago because of his physical play.

"I got a kid in the first round who is the best bodychecker I've ever seen," gushed Sudbury

"To me, it just seemed natural to hit," says the twenty-six-year-old Peca.

tapped on the shoulder by his boss and instructed to target the biggest threats on the ice.

"If it's Philadelphia, he plays one-on-one with Eric Lindros," says Ruff. "If it's Pittsburgh, it's Jaromir Jagr. If it's New Jersey, it's Jason Arnott. Size doesn't matter with Peca."

No, size does not matter for the boy from Ontario, who says he's always played with "reckless abandon" and genuinely enjoys leveling the opposition. And how does Peca respond when his opponents confront him face-to-face and threaten to deliver some punishing abuse of their own? Simply and concisely.

"Not if I get you first," he'll reply.

#27 MICHAEL PECA • Buffalo Sabres • Center

			REGULAR SEASON					PLAYOFFS				
YEAR	TEAM	LEA	GP	G	A	TP	PIM	GP	G	A	TP	PIM
1990–91	Sudbury	OHL	62	14	27	41	24	5	1	0	1	7
1991–92	Sudbury	OHL	39	16	34	50	61	.....	.....	.....	.....	.....
	Ottawa	OHL	27	8	17	25	32	11	6	10	16	6
1992–93	Ottawa	OHL	55	38	64	102	80	.....	.....	.....	.....	.....
	Hamilton	AHL	9	6	3	9	11	.....	.....	.....	.....	.....
1993–94	Ottawa	OHL	55	50	63	113	101	17	7	22	29	30
	Vancouver	NHL	4	0	0	0	2	.....	.....	.....	.....	.....
1994–95	Syracuse	AHL	35	10	24	34	75					
	Vancouver	NHL	33	6	6	12	30	5	0	1	1	8
1995–96	Buffalo	NHL	68	11	20	31	67	.....	.....	.....	.....	.....
1996–97	Buffalo	NHL	79	20	29	49	80	10	0	2	2	8
1997–98	Buffalo	NHL	61	18	22	40	57	13	3	2	5	8
1998–99	Buffalo	NHL	82	27	29	56	81	21	5	8	13	18
1999–00	Buffalo	NHL	73	20	21	41	67	5	0	1	1	4

IF THERE WAS ONE THING CHRIS Pronger learned long ago, it was this: it isn't fun to lose.

He's known that since he was barely old enough to be in school. There he'd be, playing on the street outside his house in Dryden, Ontario, or at the outdoor rink two blocks away and one thing would be clear to him—he had to win the game.

"I don't know where I get it, but I just don't like losing," recalls the burly St. Louis defenseman. "I always have been a poor sport when it comes to losing . . . from the time I was six years old I hated losing."

Pronger, who admits that he was "a little bit of a hellion" as a kid (thus earning him the nickname Chaos), says his competitive nature often led to scraps with his friends and older brother Sean. "Yeah, we killed each other a bit," he says. "That was the saying

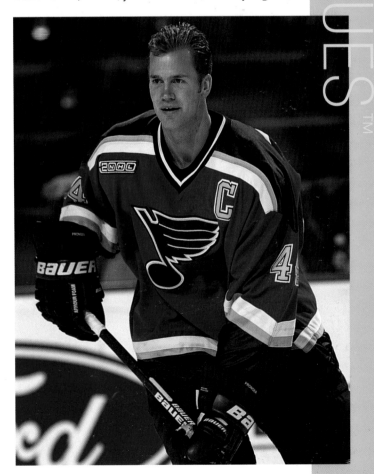

ST. LOUIS BLUES™

back home: 'There go the Pronger boys again!'" Most times, the scuffles were in fun, but once in awhile things would get carried away.

"You'd get the odd bloody nose," remembers Pronger. "You'd just have to lay in the snow for a minute, let it stop, and get back out there." Pronger is still the kind of guy who wants to get back out there—his drive to win is as intense as it's ever been. As one of the National Hockey League's top defenseman, the twenty-five-year-old Blues captain is infused, more than ever, with the competitive stuff that powered him as a boy.

It has helped, of course, that the boy grew into a rather formidable man. Calling Chris Pronger big is a little like calling an ice rink cool. He's a towering six six and weighs in at 220 pounds.

"You can beat him," says defensive teammate Al MacInnis. "But his reach is so incredible, you'll have a hard time doing it. If you get by him, he can use his stick to hook and recover. He's become such a good skater, coupled with his size, that it's almost impossible to get around him." Because he is so quick to adapt, Pronger's journey to the big leagues has been, for the most part, a smooth one.

He started playing the game at the age of five, after a year of skating lessons, and was immediately noted for his agility and coordination. Before long, people began to see something else: that unflagging competitive streak.

"Playing Atom hockey, kids aren't obviously going to be as good," says Pronger. "These kids are six, seven years old, and I'm out there screaming and hollering. Kids were scared of me because I'd get so mad. You learn from stuff like that."

In his early days, Pronger played center and one season scored 130 goals. By second year Atom, however, he made the move to the blue-line, a move that would pay off in the long run.

By the time Pronger was in his teens, he was noticed big-time—in spite of the fact that he was cut, at the age of sixteen, from the All-Ontario under-seventeen program, only to end up making the team on a wild card berth. Pronger would eventually play with the Peterborough Petes of the Ontario Hockey League, where he would help lead the team to the Memorial Cup final. He has played on the gold medal-winning Canadian world junior team, been named Canadian Hockey League defenseman of the year (1992–1993), and represented Canada at the 1998 Winter Olympics.

His achievements are many. Still, there is one achievement—and one day—that stands apart from the others, that will always be unforgettable to Pronger.

"It would probably be the NHL draft in 1993

[when Hartford picked up Pronger second overall] because I had all my family and friends there . . . Growing up, only a few kids get that opportunity to get to that level, and that happened for me."

It also happened for another of Chris' former street hockey mates: his brother Sean, who ended up playing center for the Mighty Ducks of Anaheim.

Chris, meantime, played two seasons in Hartford before being traded, in July 1995, to St. Louis for Brendan Shanahan. In many ways, the move was an enormous challenge for Pronger: the personable Shanahan had been adored by the St. Louis faithful. Pronger realized that his skates would be hard to fill.

But Pronger overcame that difficult introduction and, today, his fans embrace him. In September 1997, Pronger became the youngest captain in the Blues' thirty-year history. In 1997–1998, he finished first in the NHL's plus-minus rating with a +47. The next season, he scored 13 goals and added 33 assists for a point total of 46.

Pronger's brilliant play on the blueline last season as well as his overall leadership abilities were recognized by the NHL in the boldest of terms. Not only did Pronger win the Norris Trophy as the league's best defenseman, he also beat out Jaromir Jagr and Pavel Bure for the Hart Trophy, given to the most valuable player in the league.

Pronger was the first defenseman since Bobby Orr in 1972 to win the Hart.

"I'm honored," said Pronger upon receiving the award.

The honor was, in fact, the NHL's.

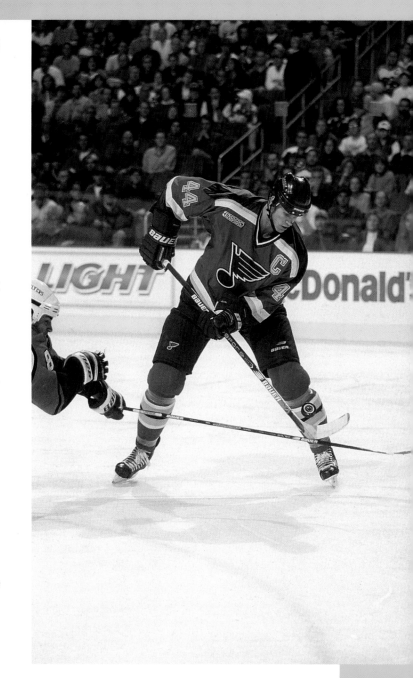

#44 CHRIS PRONGER • St. Louis Blues • Defense

			REGULAR SEASON					PLAYOFFS				
YEAR	TEAM	LEA	GP	G	A	TP	PIM	GP	G	A	TP	PIM
1991–92	Peterborough	OHL	63	17	45	62	90	10	1	8	9	28
1992–93	Peterborough	OHL	61	15	62	77	108	21	15	25	40	51
1993–94	Hartford	NHL	81	5	25	30	113	.....	.....	.....	.....	.....
1994–95	Hartford	NHL	43	5	9	14	54	.....	.....	.....	.....	.....
1995–96	St. Louis	NHL	78	7	18	25	110	13	1	5	6	16
1996–97	St. Louis	NHL	79	11	24	35	143	6	1	1	2	22
1997–98	St. Louis	NHL	81	9	27	36	180	10	1	9	10	26
	Canada Olympics		6	0	0	0	4	.....	.....	.....	.....	.....
1998–99	St. Louis	NHL	67	13	33	46	113	13	1	4	5	28
1999–00	St. Louis	NHL	79	14	48	62	92	7	3	4	7	32

#97 Jeremy Roenick

AS JEREMY ROENICK SEES IT, THERE'S a lot of truth to the old adage that nice guys finish last. In hockey anyway, it doesn't help to be Mr. Congeniality. Good guys may win popularity contests, but they don't always win hockey games.

"I don't want to be known as the nice guy and a fun guy to play against," says the Phoenix Coyotes star center. "I want to be the guy that goes out there and puts a little question mark in people's heads, not knowing what I'm going to do. When my career is over, I want to be known as a warrior, a winner, a guy that gave everything he had."

Right now, Roenick the warrior is indeed giving the game his all. The wily Coyote,

points, and making money. I admit it," he says candidly. "There was definitely a time when I didn't care whether we won or lost. If I scored a goal and had a good game, I was satisfied."

Those times, however, are in the past. Today, the thirty-year-old native of Boston, Massachusetts, is the consummate team player. Yes, he wants to win. But he also knows it takes a team to do that.

"I want people to realize that I'm a team guy and only want what's best for the Phoenix Coyotes. What's important to me is that my teammates know I'm dedicated to them and I'm dedicated to winning the Stanley Cup."

Amazingly, the Coyotes have been doing a much improved job of impressing the folks at the America West Arena since Roenick made an attitude adjustment. In the years since Roenick's been with the team, the Coyotes have made the playoffs four times. "I really love what I'm seeing from J.R. this year," says Phoenix captain Keith Tkachuk. "He really has done the job, putting the team first and foremost, and it's paying off. We're playing well, the team is playing well, and everybody is getting rewarded."

Former Coyote Murray Baron says Roenick is as strong and skilled a player as he ever was, but there are definite changes in the way he plays the game. "You're not sure exactly what to expect from him out there. He's not all over the ice anymore like he used to be, but he still has that speed and creativity and he's capable of unleashing that side of his game. He's definitely playing a more disciplined game now."

In other words, Roenick may have become precisely the kind of player he's always longed to be: tough, fast, and somewhat unpredictable. "I would like to be thought of as a guy who's going to compete as a talented player, one who you're going to have to look out for, offensively and physically," he says.

Jeremy Roenick, it seems, is a player who's arrived—and that can only be good news for the hockey fans in Phoenix.

"I'm having fun again," he says. "And I'm doing all the right things."

who finished on top of the team scoring race with 34 goals and added 44 assists for 78 points last season, has become the player he wants to be. Tough. Aggressive. A bit of a pain-in-the-neck.

And, yes, a scoring machine as well. Roenick, in fact, has put more pucks in the net than most kids have put pennies in the piggy bank. Three times he netted 100 points for the Chicago Blackhawks, the team he played with for eight years before moving to Phoenix in 1996.

He didn't sustain those numbers when he first arrived in the Valley of the Sun, but lately things have changed. Roenick has developed a new attitude toward hockey, and it's producing big results.

"There was a time in my career when all I cared about was just scoring goals, scoring

"When my career is over, I want to be known as a warrior, a winner, a guy that gave everything he had."

#97 JEREMY ROENICK • Phoenix Coyotes • Center

YEAR	TEAM	LEA	REGULAR SEASON					PLAYOFFS				
			GP	G	A	TP	PIM	GP	G	A	TP	PIM
1988–89	Hull	QMJHL	28	34	36	70	14	.....	.....	.....	.....	.....
	Chicago	NHL	20	9	9	18	4	10	1	3	4	7
1989–90	Chicago	NHL	78	26	40	66	54	20	11	7	18	8
1990–91	Chicago	NHL	79	41	53	94	80	6	3	5	8	4
1991–92	Chicago	NHL	80	53	50	103	98	18	12	10	22	12
1992–93	Chicago	NHL	84	50	57	107	86	4	1	2	3	2
1993–94	Chicago	NHL	84	46	61	107	125	6	1	6	7	2
1994–95	Koln	Ger.	3	3	1	4	2	.....	.....	.....	.....	.....
	Chicago	NHL	33	10	24	34	14	8	1	2	3	16
1995–96	Chicago	NHL	66	32	35	67	109	10	5	7	12	2
1996–97	Phoenix	NHL	72	29	40	69	115	6	2	4	6	4
1997–98	Phoenix	NHL	79	24	32	56	103	6	5	3	8	4
1998–99	Phoenix	NHL	78	24	48	72	130	1	0	0	0	0
1999–00	Phoenix	NHL	75	34	44	78	102	5	2	2	4	10

Brendan Shanahan

SOME ATHLETES ARE REVERED BY their fans because of the way they throw a ball or fire a puck. Some are adored because they're funny, smart, or entertaining.

A rare few are loved for all three.

Brendan Shanahan, as most hockey fans know, is one of those exceptions. The Detroit left winger may have a menacing shot and an outstanding point record, but he also has a wit that most comedians would die for. The fact that readers of the *Detroit Free Press* voted him their leading sports figure last year may, in fact, have as much to do with the guy's personality as his prowess on the ice.

He reads poetry. He watches *Jeopardy* in the dressing room. He loves to spin a yarn—okay, occasionally he will tell an outright lie—and claims to have run with the bulls in Pamplona, served as a ballboy at the U.S.

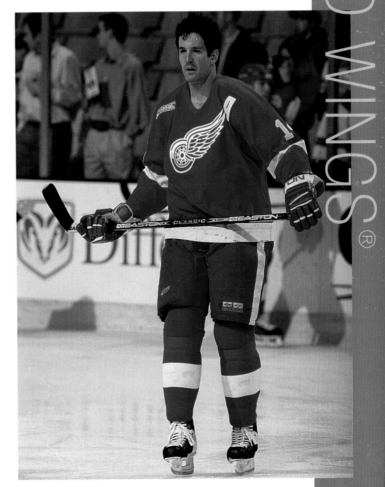

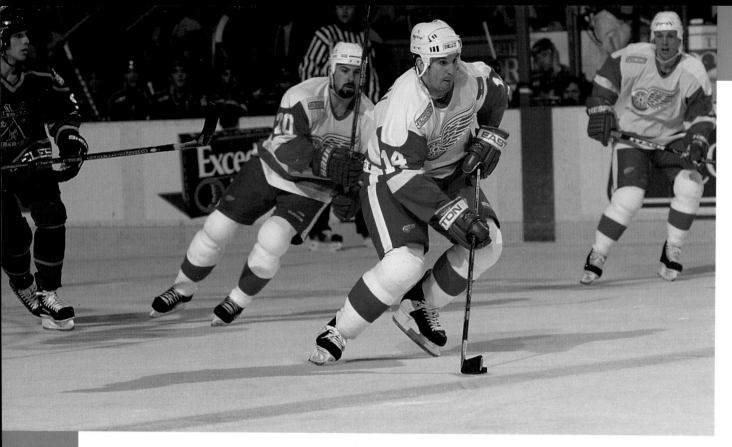

Open, and auditioned for *The Flintstones* movie.

When asked by Detroit hockey commentator Ken Daniels whether he had any game-day rituals, Shanahan responded in characteristic form. "I get up, kick the dog in both hind legs, spill milk on the floor and run my key across one side of my car, then the other, before driving to the rink." In short, he's a media darling, an athlete with good looks who's so quotable reporters almost crawl over one another to stick a microphone in his face.

That's not to say, however, that Brendan Shanahan is all fun and games.

He's also a committed hockey player with an outstanding resume. Shanahan, who hails from Mimico, Ontario, was born thirty-one years ago to Irish immigrants. He was one of four boys, arriving last and six years behind his next oldest brother. The birth order, says Shanahan, played a big part in how he developed. "The guys I emulated growing up in sports were my brothers, the way they played," recalls the Red Wing. "There was a big age gap

between me and them. They were all grouped together. They all played sports together and I was kind of like their rink rat, their ball boy in lacrosse, or their tape fetcher in hockey."

He also learned quickly that he had to be wily if he wanted to play among brothers Danny, Brian and Shaun. "I think probably, playing against my older brothers, I had to find a trick or two because they were bigger and stronger. I had to be sneaky in a way because I couldn't beat them straight up."

The tricks he learned are with him still. Shanahan learned early on that survival on the ice rink meant he would have to be creative with the puck, one of his trademarks.

Shanahan, who's known for, among other things, his incredible memory—he can tell you every detail of his first or 400th career goal, not to mention the plots of every book he read last year—made his entry into the National Hockey League in 1987, when New Jersey picked him second overall.

He was with the New Jersey Devils for four years before signing with St. Louis in 1991 as a free agent. Shanahan scored 51 goals in his second season with the Blues and 52 in the third. In 1995 he packed his bags again, this time for Hartford.

As it turns out, Shanahan's stay in Hartford

He's a media darling, an athlete with good looks who's so quotable reporters almost crawl over one another to stick a microphone in his face.

was more of a stopover; he was in Detroit a year later. The move was precipitated in part by a meeting between Red Wings captain Steve Yzerman and his coach Scotty Bowman, who wanted to know the captain's opinion of Shanahan. "If you get a chance to get this guy," Yzerman told him, "do everything you can."

Bowman did. He ended up paying a high price for Shanahan—giving up Paul Coffey, Keith Primeau, and a first-round draft choice— but the Red Wings have never regretted the move. In addition to adding personality to the club, Shanahan has also helped the Red Wings win two Stanley Cups. "A lot of guys have talent, but they don't have that extra ingredient to make them winners," says former Red Wing Ted Lindsay, the top scorer in 1950. "Brendan's got it. Stevie recognized it, and he made a great recommendation to get him. I respect that."

Today, Shanahan is as much on his game as he's ever been. He still has one of the most powerful, accurate shots in the league, and he's definitely regarded—by fans and teammates alike—as one of the most valued, likeable figures ever to don a Red Wing jersey. That, without a doubt, is even more impressive than a cameo appearance in *The Flintsones*.

#14 BRENDAN SHANAHAN • Detroit Red Wings • Left Wing

			REGULAR SEASON					PLAYOFFS			
YEAR	TEAM	LEA	GP	G	A	TP	PIM	GP	G	A	TP	PIM
1985–86	London	OHL	59	28	34	62	70	5	5	5	10	5
1986–87	London	OHL	56	39	53	92	92	.....	.....	.....	.....	.....
1987–88	New Jersey	NHL	65	7	19	26	131	12	2	1	3	44
1988–89	New Jersey	NHL	68	22	28	50	115	.....	.....	.....	.....	.....
1989–90	New Jersey	NHL	73	30	42	72	137	6	3	3	6	20
1990–91	New Jersey	NHL	75	29	37	66	141	7	3	5	8	12
1991–92	St. Louis	NHL	80	33	36	69	171	6	2	3	5	14
1992–93	St. Louis	NHL	71	51	43	94	174	11	4	3	7	18
1993–94	St. Louis	NHL	81	52	50	102	211	4	2	5	7	4
1994–95	Duseldorf	Ger.	3	5	3	8	4	.....	.....	.....	.....	.....
	St. Louis	NHL	45	20	21	41	136	5	4	5	9	14
1995–96	Hartford	NHL	74	44	34	78	125	.....	.....	.....	.....	.....
1996–97	Hartford	NHL	2	1	0	1	0	.....	.....	.....	.....	.....
	Detroit	NHL	79	46	41	87	131	20	9	8	17	43
1997–98	Detroit	NHL	75	28	29	57	154	20	5	4	9	22
	Canada Olympic		6	2	0	2	0	.....	.....	.....	.....	.....
1998–99	Detroit	NHL	81	31	27	58	123	10	3	7	10	6
1999–00	Detroit	NHL	78	41	37	78	105	9	3	2	5	10

MATS SUNDIN'S DAD MADE IT TO junior as a goalie—and that could be why his son made it to the National Hockey League as a star center. "My brothers [Patrick and Per] and I used to take shots at him at home," Sundin recalls of his childhood days in Bromma. Practicing on an experienced goaltender at a young age helped make young Mats a sniper from the word "go." He expected to score every time he was out on the ice. And he expected to win.

When his team didn't, Mats wasn't much fun to be around. "When we'd lose a game, I thought my whole world was coming apart," recalls Sundin. "I couldn't handle it." But it's fair to say that nearly every team the talented

Swede has been part of has won more often than it has lost.

Sundin would eventually leave his homeland for the bright lights and riches of the National Hockey League. And his entry into the league was one of the most heralded for a European player and partially set the stage for the flood of players that make the voyage from Sweden, Finland and the countries of Eastern Europe to make the NHL one of the most cosmopolitan sports leagues in the world.

At six four and 230 pounds, Sundin entered the NHL history books as the first European player ever picked first overall in the NHL Entry Draft. That was in 1989 when he was taken by the Quebec Nordiques. Sundin would play four years in Quebec before he was involved in a trade that would change his hockey life forever.

The Toronto Maple Leafs landed Sundin in exchange for their captain, the popular Wendel Clark, and Sylvain Lefebvre. While a first overall draft choice is always under the media microscope, the focus on Sundin would get even stronger when the Leafs made him their captain in 1997.

"You know what leadership is when you walk into the room and see four people sitting around one person," says Ken Dryden, the Leafs articulate team president. "That person that's being sat around is the leader. And that's Mats."

The sixteenth captain in the Leafs fabled history, Sundin was the first non-Canadian to hold the honor. He was succeeding one of the most popular players to ever wear the 'C' in Toronto—Doug Gilmour.

Playing in a hockey town where the expectations for success are so great and the criticism that comes with failure is swift, Sundin has known both success and failure while playing in a Maple Leafs uniform. But Sundin wouldn't trade his spot with anyone.

"Toronto is the greatest hockey city in the world," Sundin said at last year's NHL All-Star game, which was hosted by Toronto. "There is no greater place in the world to be a player and there is no other place that I'd rather play."

Sundin's ten years in Canada as an NHL player have also had a profound influence on the feelings he has for the country he calls home ten months of the year.

"I probably feel as much Canadian as Swedish," says Sundin. "I consider Canada as much my home as Sweden. I have a cottage in Sweden, but the only time I spend there is a couple of months in the summer. Most of my friends are Canadian."

Despite his success as a scorer—he had a 114-point season with Quebec in 1992–93—Sundin has constantly had to shrug off the North American stereotype of the Swedish hockey player, that he doesn't like the physical stuff.

"I can hit people," says Sundin. "I do hit people. I am never going to be a Wendel Clark like he was [in his prime], hitting and fighting everybody. That's not me. I've never played that way and I'll never be that style of hockey player. I've always thrown the hit when it's there, but I'm not going to be a player who runs out of position just to make the hit and try to get the people in the stands to cheer."

Last season, Sundin's Leafs were bounced in the second round of the playoffs. It was a huge disappointment, considering that the team had made it to the Eastern Conference finals a year earlier. Sundin knows that the pressure on him won't let up until he leads the Leafs to the promised land.

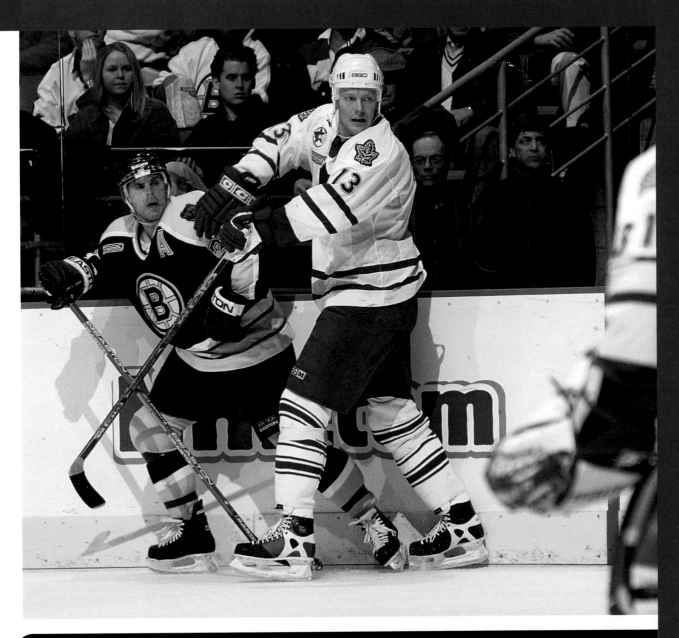

#13 MATS SUNDIN • Toronto Maple Leafs • Center

			REGULAR SEASON					PLAYOFFS				
YEAR	TEAM	LEA	GP	G	A	TP	PIM	GP	G	A	TP	PIM
1988–89	Nacka	Swe. 2	25	10	8	18	18	......	.....	.....	......	.....
1989–90	Djurgarden	Swe.	34	10	8	18	16	8	7	0	7	4
1990–91	Quebec	NHL	80	23	36	59	58	.....	.....	......	......	.....
1991–92	Quebec	NHL	80	33	43	76	103	.....	.....	......	......	.....
1992–93	Quebec	NHL	80	47	67	114	96	6	3	1	4	6
1993–94	Quebec	NHL	84	32	53	85	60	......	......	......	......	.....
1994–95	Djurgarden	Swe.	12	7	2	9	14	......	......	......	......	.....
	Toronto	NHL	47	23	24	47	14	7	5	4	9	4
1995–96	Toronto	NHL	76	33	50	83	46	6	3	1	4	4
1996–97	Toronto	NHL	82	41	53	94	59					
1997–98	Toronto	NHL	82	33	41	74	49					
	Winter Olympics		4	3	0	3	4	......	......	......	......	.....
1998–99	Toronto	NHL	82	31	52	83	58	17	8	8	16	16
1999–00	Toronto	NHL	73	32	41	73	46	12	3	5	8	10

Pierre Turgeon

PIERRE TURGEON HAS ACCUMULATED countless wonderful memories in his thirty-one years, but there's one memory that tends to stand on its own.

It was on March 11, 1996, the day the Montreal Forum closed its doors. Turgeon, a native of Quebec, understood the significance of the grand old arena. Because he was captain of the Montreal Canadiens at the time, Turgeon was given a special assignment that night.

"I got to carry the torch," recalls Turgeon. "All the captains were there and they were

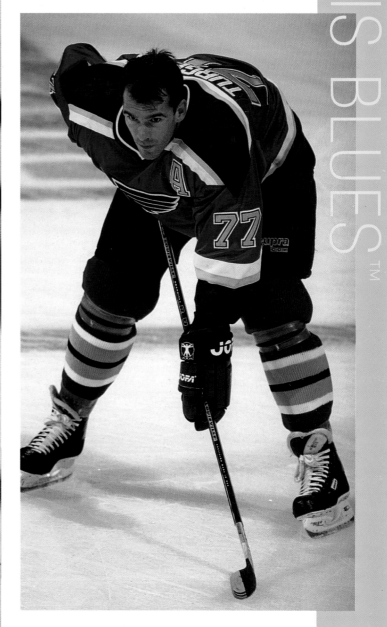

moving the torch around. The night we closed the Forum was just an unbelievable night in Montreal. Especially when you're from Quebec—and you know what the Forum means to people in Montreal. That night was something I won't forget the rest of my life."

This memory, of course, had many more to compete with. Turgeon, a six one center who now routinely gets the fans to their feet at the Kiel Centre in St. Louis, is also unlikely to forget the summer day in 1987 when he was picked first overall by the Buffalo Sabres in the NHL Entry Draft.

He won't forget winning the Lady Byng Trophy in 1993, or his ten trips to the Stanley Cup playoffs, or his last full year with the Montreal Canadiens, the year he happened to post 38 goals and 58 assists to record a staggering 96 points. He won't forget the night in 1999 when he joined that elite group of professional hockey players to break the 1,000-point barrier.

Yes, Pierre Turgeon has plenty in the memory bank.

"My main thing was [always] playing hockey," says the father of four, digging back through his childhood. "I enjoyed playing baseball, but baseball lasted just two months. It was short. It was just a good experience when I was young."

It may be somewhat of an understatement, however, to describe Turgeon's 1982 baseball season simply as a "good experience." "Amazing" would be more like it. That was the year Turgeon's all-star team, drawn from Quebec's Rouyn-Noranda area, began to win. Big-time.

Turgeon, whose team included three other kids—Stephane Matteau, Eric Desjardins and Andre Racicot—who would all, amazingly, also make it to the NHL, eventually progressed to the Canadian Little League championships and then to the Little League World Series in Williamsport, Pennsylvania.

"Our town had like 15,000–18,000 people and we put together this team," says Turgeon. "We won like three tournaments before we

went to Williamsport. I mean, we represented Canada. Back home, from what I heard, people weren't walking in the streets without a radio. Everybody had a radio."

It was Turgeon who would step up to the plate in the Canadian title game against Glace Bay, Nova Scotia. Seventh inning, two outs, and Turgeon smacks the game-tying home run.

"Pierre hit a home run, tied the game, and we went into overtime," recalls former teammate Matteau. "He scored the winning goals, uh, the winning run in the extra inning."

Turgeon, who stood five eleven back then, easily the biggest twelve-year-old in the tournament, was the star of a quarterfinal game in the World Series: he struck out twelve batters in a 3–0 win over Madrid. In the semifinal, the boys from Quebec went down to Taiwan.

It was, says Turgeon, an incredible experience—and one he seems determined to improve upon as a professional athlete. All three of the future NHL players on his team would end up winning a Stanley Cup—Desjardins and Racicot in Montreal and Matteau with the New York Rangers—and that's definitely something Turgeon aspires to do.

"The one thing I want to do is win the Stanley Cup," he says candidly. "Obviously, I would want to win the Stanley Cup."

As Turgeon has demonstrated over and over again, all goals are achievable. His level of skill, which former Montreal linemate Mark Recchi has described as "one of the tops in the league," has frequently touched stardom. In the Quebec Major Junior League, where Turgeon played for Granby, he accumulated 154 points in 1986–87. In Buffalo, Turgeon racked up 315 points in four seasons; in two of his four seasons with the New York Islanders, he posted an amazing 226 points. Turgeon, a perennial guest at the NHL All-Star game, has been in St. Louis since 1996. He is an athlete who has accomplished much, though one goal remains.

"We have something going here," he believes. "A lot of things are positive. I think we could do something."

"The one thing I want to do is win the Stanley Cup."

#77 PIERRE TURGEON • St. Louis Blues • Center

			REGULAR SEASON					PLAYOFFS				
YEAR	TEAM	LEA	GP	G	A	TP	PIM	GP	G	A	TP	PIM
1984–85	Bourassa	QAAA	41	49	52	101	.....	.....	.....	.....	.....	.....
1985–86	Granby	QMJHL	69	47	67	114	31	.....	.....	.....	.....	.....
1986–87	Granby	QMJHL	58	69	85	154	8	7	9	6	15	15
1987–88	Buffalo	NHL	76	14	28	42	34	6	4	3	7	4
1988–89	Buffalo	NHL	80	34	54	88	26	5	3	5	8	2
1989–90	Buffalo	NHL	80	40	66	106	29	6	2	4	6	2
1990–91	Buffalo	NHL	78	32	47	79	26	6	3	1	4	6
1991–92	Buffalo	NHL	8	2	6	8	4	.....	.....	.....	.....	.....
	NY Islanders	NHL	69	38	49	87	16	.....	.....	.....	.....	.....
1992–93	NY Islanders	NHL	83	58	74	132	26	11	6	7	13	0
1993–94	NY Islanders	NHL	69	38	56	94	18	4	0	1	1	0
1994–95	NY Islanders	NHL	34	13	14	27	10	.....	.....	.....	.....	.....
	Montreal	NHL	15	11	9	20	4	.....	.....	.....	.....	.....
1995–96	Montreal	NHL	80	38	58	96	44	6	2	4	6	2
1996–97	Montreal	NHL	9	1	10	11	2	.....	.....	.....	.....	.....
	St. Louis	NHL	69	25	49	74	12	5	1	1	2	2
1997–98	St. Louis	NHL	60	22	46	68	24	10	4	4	8	2
1998–99	St. Louis	NHL	67	31	34	65	36	13	4	9	13	6
1999–00	St. Louis	NHL	52	26	40	66	8	7	0	7	7	0

The Young Guns

AFINOGENOV—IT'S HARD TO SAY, BUT we'd better learn how to pronounce it. The name, after all, seems destined to become a big one.

Maxim Afinogenov, the Buffalo Sabres star rookie, is already in the process of putting the family name in lights. But then so is sister Katia, a teenage tennis prodigy who has been described as the best player of her age in the world.

"The genes in that family are just frightening," says Rick Macci, who runs the Fort Lauderdale tennis academy which Katia attends. Frightening, maybe. Incredible, for sure.

In many ways, it seems only natural that the kids from Moscow should possess superior

athletic ability. Their mom, Raisa, was a seven-time track champion in the 800 meters who was expected to compete in the 1980 Moscow Summer Olympics but missed the event because she was pregnant with Maxim. Father Sergei also excelled at sport; he played some hockey but, like Raisa, discovered that he shone brightest on the track.

Little wonder, then, that their children would inherit their gifts. Like his little sister, Twenty-one-year-old Maxim is known for his power,

speed and grace. He is a newcomer to the big leagues—a rookie who's barely learned to speak English—yet already he's been compared to that other great Russian hockey player, Pavel Bure. Both players, in fact, are right wingers who shoot left. Both seem capable of achieving tremendous speed in no time at all. And both are of a similar stature—Bure is five ten and 190 pounds, while Afinogenov is five eleven and 185. Some say they even look like brothers.

"His mannerisms remind me of Bure," says Sabres coach Lindy Ruff. "He has the same skating style. He has explosiveness to his stride. I wouldn't put him in that class yet, but he's got potential. His skating is with the elite and his stickhandling is with the elite. You combine that with the grit we've already seen and we're talking about a complete package."

This so-called "complete package" was picked by Buffalo in the third round of the 1997 Entry Draft. But the Sabres decided not to use Afinogenov right away, opting instead to send him to Rochester of the American Hockey League to become acquainted with North American-style hockey.

He wasn't there for long, however. Afinogenov led all AHL rookies by scoring 6 goals and 12 assists in his first 15 games in Rochester. The numbers would be enough to convince the Sabres that Afinogenov was ready for a promotion—as would his play at the 1999 World Junior Championship, which earned him a gold medal and recognition as the tournament's top forward.

It was in November of the same year that Afinogenov made his National Hockey League debut. The Sabres, who had been struggling in the season's early weeks, were in dire need of some scoring, so they summoned the rookie from Rochester.

As luck would have it, Afinogenov's mom was in the stands that night. Maxim scored a goal. In Afinogenov's second outing, he scored again. And in his fifth game he did one better: he scored twice. By the time he'd played 19 games with Buffalo, the rookie Russian had 8 goals, 6 assists, and a fan club that was growing by the hour.

"Max pulls a lot of tricks out of his bag," says Sabres winger Geoff Sanderson. "He's got the sweet hands and the sweet moves and he loves to dance. And he likes to beat guys more than once. He beats you once and he comes back and beats you again. It's great to watch."

Rob Ray, who also plays wing for the Sabres, feels the same way. Afinogenov, he suggests, is the kind of hockey player who seems to come from a different planet.

"When you see a player like that, you just stare at him," says Ray. "It's the same when you're watching Gretzky or Lemieux or somebody like that. You wonder, 'How do they do that?'"

In the end, it may have been good genes—or just old-fashioned hard work—that earned Afinogenov a healthy first-year point total of 34 on 16 goals and 18 assists, enough to make him one of the top rookie point-getters in the league.

Afinogenov—it may be tough to say but we'll undoubtedly get used to it.

#61 MAXIM AFINOGENOV • Buffalo Sabres • Right Wing

			REGULAR SEASON					PLAYOFFS				
YEAR	TEAM	LEA	GP	G	A	TP	PIM	GP	G	A	TP	PIM
1995–96	Mosc. D'amo	Rus-2				Statistics Not Available						
	Mosc. D'amo	CIS	1	0	0	0	0	.....	.....	.....	.....	.....
1996–97	Mosc. D'amo	Russia	29	6	5	11	10	4	0	2	2	0
1997–98	Russia	WJC-A	7	3	2	5	4	.....	.....	.....	.....	.....
	Mosc. D'amo	EuroHL	6	3	1	4	27	.....	.....	.....	.....	.....
	Mosc. D'amo	CIS	35	10	5	15	53	.....	.....	.....	.....	.....
1998–99	Mosc. D'amo	CIS	38	8	13	21	24	16	10	6	16	14
	Russia	WJC-A	7	3	5	8	0	.....	.....	.....	.....	.....
1999–00	Buffalo	NHL	65	16	18	34	41	5	0	1	1	2

#37

Curtis Brown

WHEN YOU GROW UP IN A TOWN THE size of Curtis Brown's, you pretty much have to make your own fun.

After all, there aren't a lot of mega movie complexes or monster shopping malls in Senlac, Saskatchewan, a farming community which is home to just one hundred people. In winter, however, there's never been a shortage of ice. And when you're a kid, especially a kid like Curtis Brown, it doesn't take you long to figure out what do with it.

You play hockey—nonstop.

"In a small town, it seems like all there is to do is play a lot of sports," says Brown, who started playing the game at the age of four. "That's all we ever did." Like most kids, Curtis latched onto the big dream, the one which had him wearing a National Hockey League jersey. But for some reason, it didn't take shape all at once. "When I was five, I looked

up to playing with the seven-year-olds. Then, when I was seven, I thought about the nine-year-olds. Pretty soon, I was thinking about junior hockey, then maybe getting drafted, then making it to the NHL."

"I was always looking up, seeing a goal."

He saw the goals—and he scored them too. In his midget year—Brown played with the Moose Jaw, Saskatchewan, AAA Warriors—he scored 35 goals in 36 games. As a Western Hockey League junior, Brown continued his winning ways in Moose Jaw, hitting the 30 point mark just 11 games into his first season. It would be enough to get him noticed and to turn the dream into reality.

In 1994, the six foot left winger became the Buffalo Sabres' second pick in the NHL Entry Draft and, suddenly, the kid from Senlac was going places. Today, the twenty-four-year-old Brown, a deeply religious athlete who's known as much for his intelligence and maturity as his on-ice agility, is touted by coaches and players alike as a reliable team player who thrives in pressure situations.

"He's handled things so much better than I could have at this age," says friend and teammate Jason Wooley. "Some guys are thrown into the fire and are able to handle it and that's Brownie."

Coach Lindy Ruff agrees.

"He's one guy who realizes the ups and downs of the game. He's just level-headed. Not a lot affects him. You can pretty much count on him every night."

Brown, who last year finished fifth in league voting for the Selke Trophy, given annually to the NHL's top defensive forward, was drafted as a left winger but later shifted to center when No. 1 pivot Pat Lafontaine was traded. The move has yielded results: Brown's production has been on the rise in each of his five years in the NHL. Last season, he ended up with 22 goals, 29 assists for 51 points. "He's a very important part of this team," says Lindy Ruff. "Some guys can do one thing or the other, or even a couple of things;

but Curtis is the complete package."

One of the most valuable aspects of Brown's play is his ability to almost sense where the puck is going, something Ruff says is a rare quality not seen in the average player.

"He can anticipate where passes are going," says the coach. "That [kind of] anticipation you can't teach. The best players in the game have it or they don't." Another quality Brown possesses, a quality which also isn't seen in every professional athlete, is his tendency to view pressure

as something completely productive.

"I look at pressure as really good," he says. "You see what you achieved the year before and it makes you more focused as an individual and as a team."

Focused, it seems, is the best way to describe the big kid from the little town. He's always had a goal in mind and never lacked clarity.

"He's just going to get better and better," says teammate Woolley. "There's no doubt in my mind. It's not going to stop here."

#37 CURTIS BROWN • Buffalo Sabres • Left Wing

			REGULAR SEASON					PLAYOFFS				
YEAR	TEAM	LEA	GP	G	A	TP	PIM	GP	G	A	TP	PIM
1992–93	Moose Jaw	WHL	71	13	16	29	30	.....	.....	.....	.....	.....
1993–94	Moose Jaw	WHL	72	27	38	65	82	.....	.....	.....	.....	.....
1994–95	Moose Jaw	WHL	70	51	53	104	63	10	8	7	15	20
	Buffalo	NHL	1	1	1	2	2	.....	.....	.....	.....	.....
1995–96	Moose Jaw	WHL	25	20	18	38	30	.....	.....	.....	.....	.....
	Canada	WJC-A	5	0	1	1	2	.....	.....	.....	.....	.....
	Prince Albert	WHL	19	12	21	33	8	18	10	15	25	18
	Buffalo	NHL	4	0	0	0	0	.....	.....	.....	.....	.....
	Rochester	AHL	.....	.....	.....	.....	.....	12	0	1	1	2
1996–97	Buffalo	NHL	28	4	3	7	18	.....	.....	.....	.....	.....
	Rochester	AHL	51	22	21	43	30	10	4	6	10	4
1997–98	Buffalo	NHL	63	12	12	24	34	13	1	2	3	10
1998–99	Buffalo	NHL	78	16	31	47	56	21	7	6	13	10
1999–00	Buffalo	NHL	74	22	29	51	42	5	1	3	4	6

#18

Tim Connolly

TIM CONNOLLY WAS LOOKING VERY much like a seasoned pro last year, even though he was the only active hockey player in the National Hockey League under the age of nineteen.

The New York Islanders' gifted center was barely out of high school when the season began. But his youth hardly showed on the ice. Connolly, who finished his rookie season with 34 points (14 goals and 20 assists), seemed completely up to the task at hand, in spite of the fact that he had broken his leg the previous February and didn't skate again until June, just weeks before training camp.

chose Connolly in the draft. "I can't believe what he's doing out there."

What's he's doing, of course, isn't remarkably different from what he's always done: attract attention.

As a youngster, and later as a standout with the Syracuse Stars, Connolly has always been focused and determined to excel. "I think he's got a pretty good head on his shoulders," says his mother, Anne. "He's analytical and he's goal-oriented. Tim always sets a goal for himself. When he reaches it, he sets another. You accomplish a lot more that way."

It's that determination—that winning drive—that's made the last couple of years something of a dream period in Connolly's career. In 1998–1999, Connolly came up with 34 goals and as many assists in just 46 games with Erie of the Ontario Hockey League. In August of 1999, he tried out for and made the Team USA Junior team. That same summer he became the first American player picked in the NHL draft and, just weeks later, was headed to training camp at Lake Placid, where he dazzled the coaches with his speed, agility and ability to create scoring opportunities.

"Now that I'm here, I feel like I'm part of the team just like any other guy," says the six foot, 186 pound Connolly. "It is amazing when you go out and play against Jaromir Jagr or Pavel Bure."

But if Connolly is still pinching himself, there are others who've been watching and left breathless by his play.

"I really enjoy watching him play," says Bryan Trottier, former Islander great, Hall of Famer, and assistant coach with the Colorado Avalanche. "From the standpoint of gift, holy cow! He's right there. You can't help but be a fan of talent like that. He'll be someone for the fans to really enjoy, hopefully, for a long time."

Connolly has even been compared to Trottier, something that makes the former Islander wince. "It's a great comparison, but the type of team is different, the number of veterans on the team, and the style of player he is. He's a lot more offensive-minded than I ever was, and more gifted offensively."

Connolly, who's described by those who know

"Sometimes," says fellow forward Mark Lawrence, "you forget he's only eighteen out there. He's making things happen." He is indeed.

The New York Islanders' gifted center was barely out of high school when the season began.

Connolly, a native of Baldwinsville, New York, was the Islanders' first pick—and fifth overall—in the 1999 Entry Draft. He was, noted the scouts, a superb stickhandler and a powerful shooter, and he had the potential to become an outstanding playmaker. He was, some said, rather like a Steve Yzerman in the making.

"He's way ahead of where I thought he would be," says Gordie Clark, the Islanders' director of player personnel and the man who him as a shy, calm-tempered young man, has been impressing everyone who's watched him—and no one more than his coach, Butch Goring.

"Nothing seems to fluster this kid," says Goring. "He's starting to be a factor on the ice, which is a little bit surprising, considering he's such a young player."

Connolly, who is slowly developing from a kid into an adult (he turned nineteen in May), has played in some 300 different hockey rinks, according to his father's estimation. These days Mike Connolly can't help but look back on the road they've traveled, even as he celebrates the place the trip has brought them to.

"I think of how fortunate we are," he says. "It [the youth hockey fraternity] is not a religion, it's like a pilgrimage. I have never experienced anything like the sharing of this thing. I just hope nobody pinches me. I can't believe this is still happening."

#18 TIM CONNOLLY • New York Islanders • Center

| YEAR | TEAM | LEA | REGULAR SEASON | | | | | PLAYOFFS | | | | |
			GP	G	A	TP	PIM	GP	G	A	TP	PIM
1997–98	Erie	OHL	59	30	32	62	32	7	1	6	7	6
1998–99	Erie	OHL	46	34	34	68	50	.....	.....	.....	.....	.....
1999–00	NY Islanders	NHL	81	14	20	34	44	.....	.....	.....	.....	.....

Chris Drury

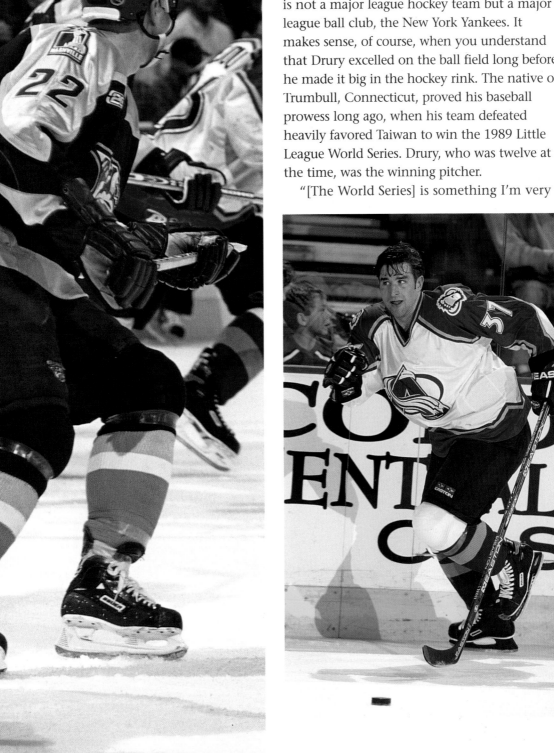

COLORADO AVALANCHE®

CHRIS DRURY MAY BE ONE OF THE most awesome young talents in the National Hockey League, but, as far as he's concerned, hockey is not the only great game going.

There's also baseball.

In fact, one of Drury's all-time favorite teams is not a major league hockey team but a major league ball club, the New York Yankees. It makes sense, of course, when you understand that Drury excelled on the ball field long before he made it big in the hockey rink. The native of Trumbull, Connecticut, proved his baseball prowess long ago, when his team defeated heavily favored Taiwan to win the 1989 Little League World Series. Drury, who was twelve at the time, was the winning pitcher.

"[The World Series] is something I'm very

proud of," says Drury. "It's a big deal in this country. Baseball in America is obviously huge." But while the baseball section of Drury's scrapbook may be impressive, the hockey pages are even better.

Drury, who last year played his second season with the Colorado Avalanche, drawing praise from everyone in the league, has amassed more than a few accolades in his twenty-four years. At thirteen, he won a state hockey championship. In 1995, he helped lead his Boston University hockey team to the NCAA title. In 1998, he won the Hobey Baker Memorial Award as the nation's top college player. That same year the feisty center signed a two-year deal with Colorado and went on to accumulate 44 points, knocking in 20 goals and adding 24 assists, and win the Calder trophy as the NHL's top rookie.

"Drury," says Avs coach Bob Hartley, "has been outstanding. He's only a young kid, but he plays with lots of intensity."

Call it intensity, call it competitive drive.

Whatever it is, it's ingrained in Chris Drury.

"I guess it's just in my blood," says Drury, who's become recognized for his relentlessly scrappy play, something not often associated with a player who stands five ten and weighs 180 pounds.

"It probably comes from being the youngest all my life. Just having to compete for every little thing at the dinner table or in football games in the back yard."

It was back in the 1994 NHL Entry Draft that Drury was selected, seventy-second overall, by the Quebec Nordiques. But rather than head to the NHL right away, he focused his attentions on the Boston University Terriers.

To say he was impressive is a gross understatement.

In his years at Boston U, the soft-spoken Drury garnered the highest individual honors ever awarded in the seventy-seven-year history of the university. He was the Terriers' all-time leading scorer, knocking in an amazing 101 goals in his final three years with the team. In his last season, the year he won the Hobey Baker, he scored 28 goals and added 29 assists.

"I can't remember coaching anybody that

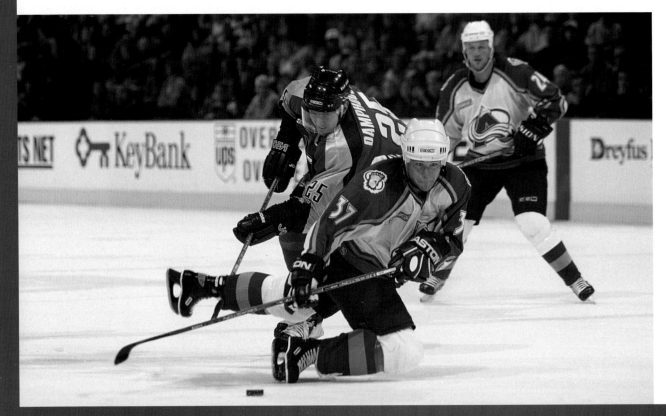

embodies the talent and competitive spirit Chris Drury has shown from his first day of practice at Boston University," said his coach at BU, Jack Parker.

"You could wake him up at three in the morning and bring him to the Boston Skating Club and tell him you're going to have a pick-up game and he would play."

Leaving the college scene and jumping to the big league—without spending time in the minors—was initially an adjustment for Drury. His routine was different, his family was far away, and his teammates, at first, were strangers.

"I didn't know what the guys were like and they didn't know me," recalls Drury. It also felt peculiar—and a little bit unworldly—to be wearing the same jersey as people like Joe

Sakic, Peter Forsberg and Patrick Roy. Before long, however, Drury was feeling like a part of the team. It helped, of course, that he quickly established himself as one of its most valuable players.

By season's end, he was a natural candidate for the Calder trophy and edged out teammate Milan Hejduk and Ottawa's Marian Hossa for the top rookie honors.

A year later, Drury continued to impress. At the end of the season he had accumulated 67 points—20 goals and 47 assists—adding more press clippings for his scrapbook.

"I have always felt, ever since I was a freshman in college," says Drury, "that if I worked as hard as I could, that good things would happen." In Drury's case, they have.

#37 CHRIS DRURY • Colorado Avalanche • Center

| YEAR | TEAM | LEA | REGULAR SEASON | | | | | PLAYOFFS | | | | |
			GP	G	A	TP	PIM	GP	G	A	TP	PIM
1993–94	Fairfield Prep	USHS	24	37	18	55	.....	.....	.....	.....	.....	.....
1994–95	Boston Univ.	H.E.	39	12	15	27	38	.....	.....	.....	.....	.....
1995–96	Boston Univ.	H.E.	37	35	33	68	46	.....	.....	.....	.....	.....
	United States	WJC-A	6	2	2	4	2	.....	.....	.....	.....	.....
1996–97	Boston Univ.	H.E.	41	38	24	62	64	.....	.....	.....	.....	.....
	United States	WC-A	8	0	1	1	2	.....	.....	.....	.....	.....
1997–98	United States	WC-A	6	1	2	3	12	.....	.....	.....	.....	.....
	Boston Univ.	H.E.	38	28	29	57	88	.....	.....	.....	.....	.....
1998–99	Colorado	NHL	79	20	24	44	62	19	6	2	8	4
1999–00	Colorado	NHL	82	20	47	67	42	17	4	10	14	4

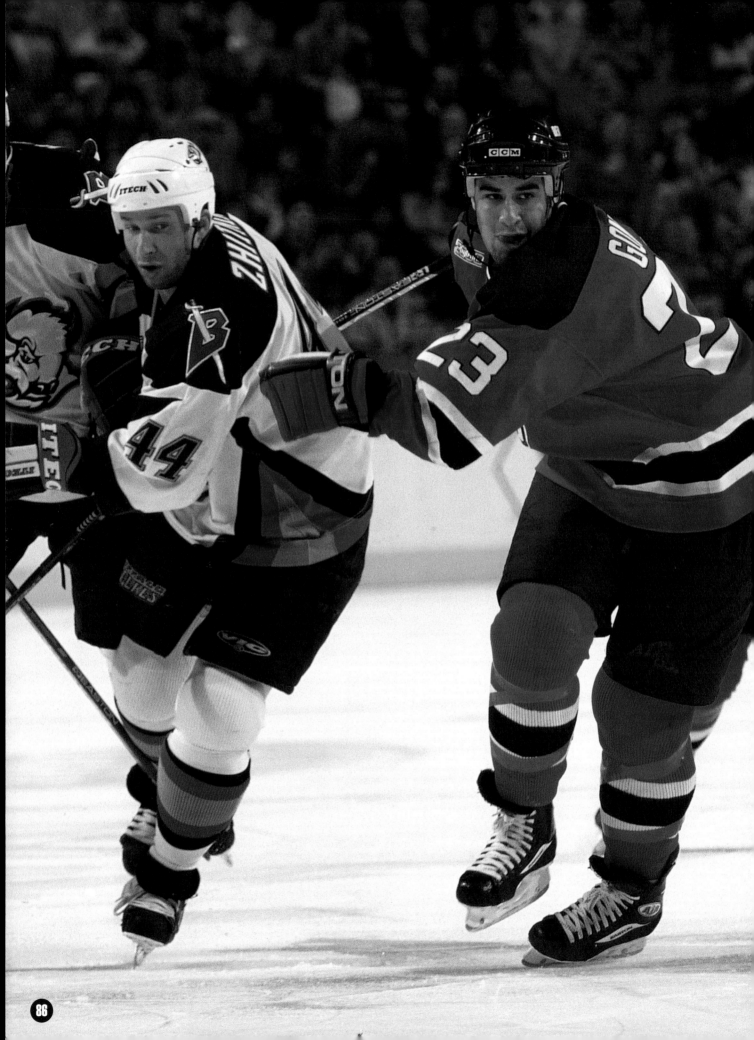

#23

Scott Gomez

SCOTT GOMEZ DIDN'T CARE MUCH FOR hockey when he first took it up. He didn't care for the wobbly feeling in his five-year-old legs when he skated on the ice. In fact, he had such little regard for the game he wanted to quit. Immediately.

But Carlos Gomez, who had spent fifty dollars on a new pair of skates for young Scott, asked his son to be patient. Finish the year, he said, and if he still didn't like hockey after it was over, they would talk. Scott Gomez did more than finish the year, he ended up skating right to the National Hockey League.

"I credit my parents for the opportunity they gave me when I was young," says the

spectacular New Jersey Devils rookie. "If it wasn't for them, I honestly wouldn't be here."

As a youngster, Gomez brought his knock-kneed, pigeon-toed walking style to the ice. At first people in his hometown of Anchorage, Alaska, talked about how odd it looked. But soon any fashion flaws were forgotten. The kid could fly. And shoot. And pass. And score. He also had a 360-degree view of the ice that teammates and opponents could only dream about.

He was a hockey prodigy.

As a teenager, Gomez played for the Tri-City Americans of the Western Hockey League. In 1998, the New Jersey Devils drafted him twenty-seventh overall in the NHL Entry Draft. He would return to junior after his first training camp, determined to make the big club the next time around. He would.

Many wondered if Gomez could have the same impact he had in junior at the pro level. He wouldn't have been the first junior star who found the NHL mountain too hard to climb. Hockey aficionados also wondered if a kid only five eleven and 190 pounds could survive among the giants now playing in the league, especially as a rookie in a new position—left wing—not the center spot he'd played all his life.

Scott Gomez didn't want to be satisfied with just making the Devils. No, that wouldn't be enough. He wanted to be the best on the team. He wanted to lead it in scoring. Preposterous? Stupid? So what! Why not try? Well, the strangest thing began to happen. He'd pass and his teammates would score. His teammates would pass and he would score. Just like it had always been.

Scott Gomez was no longer just some happy-go-lucky kid who to play hockey. He was more. All of a sudden, he was the shoe-in rookie of the year. An all-star invitee. A future superstar. And in a league concerned with its homogeneous ethnic base, Gomez was something else: the face of a minority.

Next thing you knew he was answering

> "If anyone had told me I would have a year like this, I wouldn't have believed them."

questions about being the first Hispanic player ever drafted in the first round of the NHL entry draft. "It's something I'll probably have to deal with the rest of my life, but it's not something I've thought about too much," Gomez said last season.

"In Alaska, I wasn't the Mexican hockey player, I was just a hockey player." Nonetheless, Gomez's unusual path to the NHL became a popular story among those who covered the league, a story that started with a father who was one of ten brothers of a poor Mexican family. As a young man, Carlos Gomez moved to Alaska to work on the pipeline. There he met his wife, Dalia, and the two raised a family of their own.

The Gomez family never had a lot of money, certainly not enough to cover the costs of Scott's hockey. So they found money other ways. In the summer, they operated a taco stand at the annual state fair in Palmer, Alaska. They sold pizzas. And raffle tickets. Anything. Like so many hockey parents, they made sacrifices every day of their lives to help pay the costs of their children's sporting activities.

This season it all paid off when they lived out the ultimate hockey parent's fantasy: they attended an NHL game in Madison Square Garden, where Carlos and Dalia Gomez watched their son play against the New York Rangers. Carlos even drove his son to the rink, just like he had so many times when Scott was a boy.

"I told him to just think about the things that got him there and to have fun," Carlos remembered telling his son before he left the car for the visitors dressing room. "And then I honked the horn as he walked away."

As his parents cheered on, Scott Gomez scored his first NHL hat-trick. By season's end, he would have 19 goals and 51 assists for 70 points, second on the veteran-laden Devils.

"If anyone had told me I would have a year like this, I wouldn't have believed them," said Gomez about a season that would ultimately include rookie of the year honors and a Stanley Cup. "It's unbelievable."

Which is as good a word as any to describe Scott Gomez. "Unbelievable."

#23 SCOTT GOMEZ • New Jersey Devils • Center

| YEAR | TEAM | LEA | REGULAR SEASON | | | | | PLAYOFFS | | | | |
			GP	G	A	TP	PIM	GP	G	A	TP	PIM
1996–97	Surrey	BCJHL	56	48	76	124	94	.....	.....	.....	.....	.....
1997–98	Tri-City	WHL	45	12	37	49	57	.....	.....	.....	.....	.....
	United States	WJC-A	7	1	0	1	2	.....	.....	.....	.....	.....
1998–99	Tri-City	WHL	58	30	78	108	55	10	6	13	19	31
	United States	WJC-A	6	3	7	10	4	.....	.....	.....	.....	.....
1999–00	New Jersey	NHL	82	19	51	70	78	23	4	6	10	4

WATCH MILAN HEJDUK PLAY HOCKEY and you can be forgiven if you think you're watching a veteran. After all, he plays like he's been around the big leagues for awhile— with confidence, grace and undeniable skill.

But he's no veteran at all. In fact, Hejduk is still a relative newcomer to the NHL. It was only two seasons ago, in the 1998– 1999 season, that the right winger from the Czech Republic first put on a Colorado Avalanche uniform and skated in the National Hockey League. And, yes, he scored a goal that night. He even had an assist.

"He's showing the poise of a veteran," says his coach Bob Hartley. "He's always in position and he's adjusted very well to the hockey

COLORADO AVALANCHE®

being played in North America. Give him credit. He works hard, he pays attention to little details, and he wants to improve."

Hartley isn't the only one who tends to gush a little when talking about the twenty-four-year-old Hejduk.

Ask fellow Av winger Adam Deadmarsh what he thinks about the new kid in the lineup and you'll hear the same kind of praise.

"He's a very skilled player and he does great defensively," says Deadmarsh. "He's been very consistent and he's always a threat."

Consistency earned Hejduk 48 points—14 goals and 34 assists—in his rookie year with the Avalanche. It also made him one of three finalists for the Calder trophy, given annually to the league's top rookie. (The award ended up going to teammate Chris Drury). In the playoffs that year, Hejduk was brilliant, scoring 6 goals and 6

assists in 16 games, including two overtime winners in Colorado's battle against San Jose.

Last season, Hejduk continued his winning ways, posting a remarkable sophomore year. He ended with 36 goals wins and 36 assists, play that was solid enough to earn him a berth on the World Team in his first NHL All-Star game.

Remarkable, yes, but perhaps not too surprising given that hockey has always been part of Milan Hejduk's life. His father, Milan Sr., played in the Czech elite league until an injury forced him to move from his native Pardubice to Sstnad-Labem. Hejduk's father played there until his retirement, when he turned to coaching.

When Hejduk thinks back to his early days, an ice rink often figures prominently. "When I started to play hockey, I was five-years-old or so. I spent a lot of time in the rink [watching his father coach] and right next to that there were tennis courts and my mother was a tennis player. So I spent my time on tennis and hockey."

At sixteen, Hejduk returned to his parents' home town, Pardubice. He played one year for a junior team there and then for five seasons with the top Czech league. In his final year, 1997–98, he collected 45 points in 48 games—an average of almost a point a game.

But that's not the extent of Hejduk's resume. He has played at the World Junior Championships, at the World Championships, and, in 1998, he was part of the gold medal-winning Czech Olympic team. It was when he first began to skate in North America, however, that Hejduk began to turn heads within the NHL. He was immediately impressive, in spite of the fact that he was struggling to deal with a new language, a new culture and a new style of hockey.

Today, Hejduk will tell you (in clear English) that the biggest hurdles are behind him.

"I'm more comfortable," he says. "It is the language. I know the guys better and the lifestyle, too. It's everything." Everything, of course, includes hockey. Hejduk has proven that he's not only adjusted to the North American game, he also excels at it.

Avalanche assistant coach Bryan Trottier, a Hall of Famer and six-time Stanley Cup champion, has watched Hejduk closely and says the young Czech has been compared, justifiably, to one of hockey's all-time greats, Mike Bossy.

"Milan has made some Bossy-like plays and made some plays that I think can be compared to a lot of the players," says Trottier, who played with Bossy on the New York Islanders.

"He's learning the game very fast. He's so young, too. After a little while in the league, he's going to be that much more ahead. He's going to be a very difficult player to stop. He already is."

#23 MILAN HEJDUK • **Colorado Avalanche • Right Wing**

YEAR	TEAM	LEA	REGULAR SEASON					PLAYOFFS				
			GP	G	A	TP	PIM	GP	G	A	TP	PIM
1993–94	Pardubice	Czech.	22	6	3	9	.....	10	5	1	6	.....
1994–95	Pardubice	Czech.	43	11	13	24	6	6	3	1	4	.....
1995–96	Pardubice	Czech.	37	13	7	20	.....	.....	.....	.....	.....	.....
1996–97	Pardubice	Czech.	51	27	11	38	10	10	6	0	6	27
1997–98	Czech Rep.	WC-A	1	0	0	0	0	.....	.....	.....	.....	.....
	Czech Rep.	Olympic	4	0	0	0	2	.....	.....	.....	.....	.....
	Pardubic	Czech.	48	26	19	45	20	3	0	0	0	2
1998–99	Colorado	NHL	82	14	34	48	26	16	6	6	12	4
1999–00	Colorado	NHL	82	36	36	72	16	17	5	4	9	6

Marian Hossa

OTTAWA SENATORS®

IN HOCKEY, SOME PLAYERS CREATE A stir, some create excitement and some create the kind of electricity that leaves the spectators gasping. Marian Hossa is among the electric ones.

"To know what kind of player he is," says Ottawa Senators assistant coach Perry Pearn, "all you have to do is look at the reaction of the people in Ottawa, because this is the kind of guy who lifts people out of their seats."

Perhaps it's his speed. Perhaps it's the way he hangs onto the puck. Perhaps it's the way he knocks it past the goaltender, which is quite frequently.

Whatever it is, Hossa has it—in spades. "You look at the guy," gushes Pearn, "and he

just has all kinds of tremendous assets." Indeed, he has.

It was those assets, those incredible, rare hockey instincts, that prompted Ottawa to recruit the Slovakian right winger in the 1997 Entry Draft. It was those assets that saw him record an astonishing thirty points in his rookie season, in spite of a knee injury that sidelined him for the first twenty-two games of the 1998–1999 season. And, yes, it was those very same assets that saw him named runner-up—behind Colorado's Chris Drury—for that year's Calder Trophy, awarded annually to the top newcomer in the NHL.

"He definitely has a long career ahead of him, and there's no doubt he's going to be a marquee player for this franchise," says Ottawa captain Daniel Alfredsson.

The twenty-one-year-old Hossa, who hails from Trencin, Slovakia, a textile town of about 60,000 people, says that, in many ways, his roots contributed to his growth as a hockey player. The town did not have the amenities found in many similarly sized North American

"Give Hossa time with the puck and he's going to do some magnificent things with it."

communities and athletes, including hockey players, had to make the necessary adjustments.

"In Slovakia, when you have one rink for a whole town, you must make good use of the time," he points out. "You learn to practise harder and you learn to play smarter."

It helped, of course, that Hossa came from a hockey family. His father, Frantisek, played defense for thirteen years for Dulka Trencin, part of the Slovak elite professional league, before turning his attention to coaching. His charges would include many standouts, including New York Islander star Zigmund Palffy.

Frantisek wanted Marian in skates early, and so he was—from almost the time he began walking. From then on, family life tended to revolve around the on-ice development of Marian and brother Marcel, who last season played for the Western Hockey League's Portland Winter Hawks and appears destined for the NHL.

"The family's life has been geared toward the growth of the boys," says Hossa's mother, Maria. "Hockey always came first, before anything else." Hossa also recalls it that way. "We've always been a hockey family," he says. "When I played for Trencin in the Slovakian

League, my dad coached about an hour's drive away. When [the two teams] played against each other, the local newspapers would ask my mother who she was cheering for. She always said: 'My son.'" Hossa joined Dulka Trencin when he was just seventeen and quickly proved he wasn't out of place by scoring 25 goals and 44 points in 46 games. The next season, he played in the world championships, and was drafted twelfth overall by Ottawa.

A year later, Hossa led the Senators by scoring 7 points in 7 preseason games. His coaches were impressed but felt that Hossa would benefit from increased exposure to a smaller North American ice surface, so they sent him to Portland to play for the Winter Hawks.

Hossa says the move turned out to be for the best. He scored 45 goals and added 40 assists in just 53 regular season games to lead the Hawks to the Memorial Cup. It was in the final game of the series, though, that Hossa suffered a major setback: he was injured during a collision that resulted in reconstructive knee surgery and six months of rehab.

Some players might have lost their momentum—and their passion—after sustaining such an injury, but not Hossa. He concentrated on recovery relentlessly, and, in the words of conditioning coach Randy Lee, attacked the weight room like a "madman."

"He went above and beyond what's normal, with how hard he pushed himself," recalls Lee.

"There's always a fear factor, not wanting to re-injure yourself, and once he overcame that he didn't waste any time." Hossa would return, of course, and he would do it in style. He didn't simply regain his strength, he would emerge stronger than he'd ever been before.

Hossa's brilliant puck-handling would be unaffected by the lost ice time, and no one noticed that more than former Senators goalie Ron Tugnutt.

"You're tempted to say the puck follows him, but it doesn't," says Ron Tugnutt now of the Columbus Blue Jackets. "He knows where the puck is going to go. Talented players have a knack for that. They go to the open ice and find the puck. Give Hossa time with the puck and he's going to do some magnificent things with it."

#18 MARIAN HOSSA • Ottawa Senators • Left Wing

			REGULAR SEASON					PLAYOFFS				
YEAR	TEAM	LEA	GP	G	A	TP	PIM	GP	G	A	TP	PIM
1995–96	Dulka Trencin	Slovakia Jr.	53	42	49	91	26	.....	.....	.....	.....	.....
	Slovakia '78	European	5	1	3	4	6	.....	.....	.....	.....	.....
1996–97	Dulka Trencin	Slovakia	46	25	19	44	33	7	5	5	10	.....
1997	Slovakia	WJC	6	5	2	7	2	.....	.....	.....	.....	.....
	Slovakia '77	European	2	3	0	3	0	.....	.....	.....	.....	.....
1997	Slovakia	WHC	8	0	2	2	0	.....	.....	.....	.....	.....
1997–98	Ottawa	NHL	7	0	1	1	0	.....	.....	.....	.....	.....
	Portland	WHL	53	45	40	85	50	16	13	6	19	6
1998	Slovakia	WJC	6	4	4	8	12	.....	.....	.....	.....	.....
1998–99	Ottawa	NHL	60	15	15	30	37	4	0	2	2	4
1999	Slovakia	WHC	6	5	2	7	8	.....	.....	.....	.....	.....
1999–00	Ottawa	NHL	78	29	27	56	32	6	0	0	0	2

Sami Kapanen

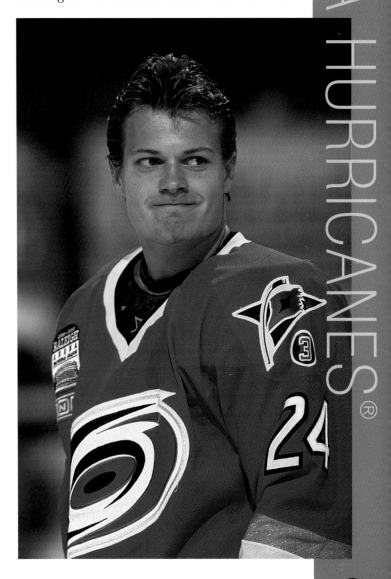

ASK ANY PROFESSIONAL HOCKEY
player who his major influences were and
you'll probably hear the usual names:
Gretzky, Trottier, Orr. Not so with Sami
Kapanen. He'd be quick to tell you that the
person who influenced him the most was
none other than his dad.

Little wonder, for Sami's father, Hannu
Kapanen, is a household name in Finland.
That's what happens when you've been a
hero on the National Team and then become
the most successful coach in the country.

It was in 1976 that Hannu Kapanen represented his country at the Olympics, narrowly
missing out on a bronze medal after his own

CAROLINA HURRICANES®

goal was disallowed. Twenty-one years later he returned to international competition, this time coaching a young Finnish team to gold at the World Junior Championships.

Even though Hannu has his own hockey concerns—he currently coaches Jokerit, one of the Finnish League's top teams—he always has time to encourage his son. And that, says Paul Maurice, coach of the Carolina Hurricanes, is evident in the way Sami plays.

"You can tell he's a coach's son because of the way he thinks on the ice and by the pressure he puts on himself," says Maurice. "Sometimes there's a real advantage when your dad's a coach . . . he knows the game. He does all the things away from the ice that tells you he's been taught well."

As a youngster growing up in Finland, Kapanen may have garnered attention because of his father's name and reputation, but he achieved stardom on his own. It was through skill and hard work that Kapanen won silver in 1994 and gold in 1995 at the World Championships. It was because of his determination that he posted 42 points in 49 games with HIFK Helsinki in 1994–1995. And it was because of Kapanen's tremendous ability that he was recruited by Hartford in the 1995 NHL Entry Draft. Since then, the twenty-six-year-old left winger has left an indelible mark on the team. It's his name and no one else's that's being chanted in the Raleigh Entertainment and Sports Arena.

"The Feisty Finn," as he's nicknamed, has averaged 25 goals and 61 points in his first two full seasons in the National Hockey League. Last season he kept up the pace, scoring 24 goals with as many assists.

Kapanen's performance not only impressed the coaches, it also earned him his first berth on the World Team in the 2000 NHL All-Star game. It was a thrill, not only because he came away

winning the fastest skater competition—clocking a time of 13.649 seconds—but because he'd always dreamed of participating in the event.

"Growing up, I'd watch the All-Star game on television and see all the big-shot players," he recalls. "You'd see the cheering fans and sense

how much fun it was, sense all the excitement." Kapanen, who grew up modeling his game after another Finnish star, Jari Kurri, has accumulated more than a handful of glowing achievements in his short career, not the least of which was a bronze medal at the 1998 Olympics in Nagano, Japan. Even so, it's his arrival in the NHL, the biggest show of them all, that gives Kapanen the greatest feeling of accomplishment.

"This league," he points out, "is the highest level of hockey in the world. I'm still young, so I think I'll be able to get better as a hockey player. I still have a lot to learn."

That may be true, but there's no denying that Kapanen has already learned a lot about the game from his coaches, his teammates, and, yes, from his dad. Coach Maurice has nothing but praise for the young winger and has described him, on more than one occasion, as his best defensive forward outside of Ron Francis, a Selke Trophy winner.

"He's very skilled," says Francis. "He's got great speed and puck-handling ability. Each and every game, each and every season, he's going to get better and better because of his work ethic and desire."

Hurricanes GM Jim Rutherford would hardly quibble with that estimate. As he sees it, Kapanen is a player who will only increase in value. "He's been a solid performer for our team over the last two-plus seasons," he says. "And we expect Sami to be an important part of our team's success in the future."

#24 SAMI KAPANEN • Carolina Hurricanes • Right Wing

| YEAR | TEAM | LEA | REGULAR SEASON | | | | | PLAYOFFS | | | | |
			GP	G	A	TP	PIM	GP	G	A	TP	PIM
1991–92	KalPa Kuopio	Finland	42	15	10	25	8	.....	.....	.....	.....	.....
1992–93	KalPa Kuopio	Finland	37	4	17	21	12	.....	.....	.....	.....	.....
1993–94	KalPa Kuopio	Finland	48	23	32	55	16	.....	.....	.....	.....	.....
1994–95	HIFK Helsinki	Finland	49	14	28	42	42	3	0	0	0	0
1995–96	Springfield	AHL	28	14	17	31	4	3	1	2	3	0
	Hartford	NHL	35	5	4	9	6	.....	.....	.....	.....	.....
1996–97	Hartford	NHL	45	13	12	25	2	.....	.....	.....	.....	.....
1997–98	Carolina	NHL	81	26	37	63	16	.....	.....	.....	.....	.....
	Finland	Olympics	6	0	1	1	0	.....	.....	.....	.....	.....
1998–99	Carolina	NHL	81	24	35	59	10	5	1	1	2	0
1999–00	Carolina	NHL	76	24	24	48	12	.....	.....	.....	.....	.....

A COUPLE OF YEARS AGO, WHEN YVON and Christianne Lecavalier were heading back to Quebec from a trip to Florida, they carried with them the most unusual souvenir.

While other folks were toting T-shirts and seashells, the Lecavaliers were returning home with something infinitely more precious: a hockey puck. It wasn't, of course, just any old hunk of rubber. Instead, it represented the culimination of a dream: it was the puck that was used by their son Vincent to score his first NHL goal.

"I'm so happy for Vincent, but I'm happy we saw it too," said Yvon of that moment in the first period when Vincent knocked the puck past Vancouver's Garth Snow to help

TAMPA BAY LIGHTNING®

"He has a confidence about him. He has that gift."

Tampa Bay secure a 3-2 victory. "I saw it go in and just went, 'Yeah!'"

After the game, Vincent wrapped the puck in masking tape and presented it to his father, who would place it among his medals, jerseys, and trophies in the basement of the family's Montreal home.

The goal, of course, was monumental but by no means unexpected. No one has ever wondered whether the Lightning center would make the scoreboard, it was just a matter of when.

For Lecavalier, Tampa Bay's celebrated No. 1 draft pick, it came on October 25, 1998, just weeks into his rookie season. His parents may have cheered the goal, but so, too, did thousands of others, the fans who happened to be in the Ice Palace that night. They had, after

all, been hearing plenty about the young superstar from Quebec, the one former Tampa Bay owner Art Williams had described—much to Lecavalier's chagrin—as the Michael Jordan of hockey.

"If he keeps maturing, he's going to be one of the great ones," says Wendel Clark, who played with Lecavalier in Tampa. "You can see it when he has the puck. He has a confidence about him. He has that gift."

The gift, of course, has been apparent for some time. At the age of only twenty, Lecavalier may still be very much "The Kid", but he's been behaving beyond his years for a long time—at least since he was fourteen, when he left home to attend Notre Dame College, a residential prep school south of Regina, Saskatchewan. Notre Dame, which has produced hockey greats such as Clark, Toronto goalie Curtis Joseph, and Carolina's Rod Brind'Amour, was Lecavalier's home for two years. After that, he traveled back to Quebec, where he would join Rimouski of the Quebec Major Junior Hockey League.

By the time he moved to Florida, Lecavalier was used to living on his own—more or less. Teammate Enrico Ciccone, a fellow French Canadian, knew that, while Lecavalier had exceptional abilities on the ice, he still needed help on the domestic front.

"I tried to teach him some things," said Ciccone. "Like washing clothes: colors go with colors, whites together, do your jeans all at the same time. That sort of thing."

Whether Lecavalier has mastered the laundry remains to be seen, but there's little doubt he's lived up to his billing on the ice. By the end of his sophomore season, he'd emerged as Tampa Bay's No. 1 man, scoring 25 goals and 42 assists for 67 points—tops on the team.

"He is so talented," says linemate Fredrik Modin. "And now he's starting to show it every night. He can do it all."

The fleet-footed center, who's gained a reputation as a superb passer with an uncanny accuracy when shooting on the net, is undoubtedly gifted physically; but he's also a standout mentally.

#4　VINCE LECAVALIER • Tampa Bay Lightning • Center

					REGULAR SEASON					PLAYOFFS			
YEAR	TEAM	LEA	GP	G	A	TP	PIM	GP	G	A	TP	PIM
1996–97	Rimouski	QMJHL	64	42	61	103	38	4	4	3	7	2
1997–98	Rimouski	QMJHL	58	44	71	115	117	18	15	26	41	46
	Canada	WJC	7	1	1	2	4	.....	.....	.....	.....	.....
1998–99	Tampa Bay	NHL	82	13	15	28	23	.....	.....	.....	.....	.....
1999–00	Tampa Bay	NHL	80	25	42	67	43	.....	.....	.....	.....	.....

David Legwand

IN MANY WAYS, HE'S YOUR AVERAGE teen. He's a big kid who loves his baseball caps, a nineteen-year-old who likes to laugh and hang out with the guys. But David Legwand is anything but ordinary. After all, few people his age can say they were drafted by the National Hockey League. Even fewer can say they were the first draft pick of a brand-new franchise.

But Legwand can. Two years ago, just before his eighteenth birthday, the native of Grosse Pointe, Michigan, became the Nashville Predators' No. 1 choice and the league's second pick overall.

"He's our future franchise player," gushes veteran Cliff Ronning, who describes

Predators coach Barry Trotz. "He can skate, shoot, he sees the ice well and he's got good puck skills." Equally important, says Trotz, is Legwand's ability to make things happen—for creating plays—in a hockey game.

"He can put people in their seats and he can bring them out of their seats," says Trotz.

All that ability, noted Nashville scouts a few years back, yielded impressive results. At seventeen, when Legwand was a star center in the Ontario Hockey League, he scored 54 goals and added 51 assists and was named the league's MVP and rookie of the year.

"He was such a dominant player on this level that he'd amaze us almost on a nightly basis," recalls Peter DeBoer, coach of the OHL Plymouth Whalers. The following season, Legwand was drafted by the NHL but ended up returning to the OHL after he was diagnozed with mononucleosis at the Predators' training camp. As it turns out, Nashville's loss was the Whalers' gain: by season's end, Legwand had collected 31 goals and 49 assists for the Michigan club.

Looking back, the flashy six two center says the extra year in the junior ranks was the best thing that could have happened. For one thing, it meant he could spend one more year living with his family, since Plymouth was in the vicinity of his parents' home.

"It was the right choice," he says. "I came to camp a lot stronger this year. It takes anyone a while to become an impact player, four or five years. The Modanos and the Jagrs didn't just step in right away and dominate."

Legwand may not have ended up dominating the Predators' play in his inaugural season, but he was hardly invisible. He posted an impressive 28 points by the end of the regular season—13 goals and 15 assists—and had won the respect of his teammates as a good-natured team player with a solid work ethic.

"He doesn't let anything affect him, get him down," says Bouchard. "He just goes out there and plays. No fuss. No complications. He's our baby. We love him. We take him with us wherever we go."

Legwand's skating and stickhandling skills as exceptional. "He's going to lead this team for a long, long time."

"He has the perfect temperament to be a superstar," adds former Calgary Flame Joel Bouchard. "He's young and full of energy. Loves life. Singing two minutes before the game."

The singing, however, was not what attracted the Predators' attention. It was the other stuff like Legwand's power, energy, and knack for putting a puck between the pipes. He is, some say, much like the Dallas Stars' powerhouse Mike Modano or Detroit captain Steve Yzerman.

"He's got all the physical tools," says

"He's young and full of energy. Loves life. Singing two minutes before the game."

DAVID LEGWAND • Nashville Predators • Center

			REGULAR SEASON					PLAYOFFS				
YEAR	TEAM	LEA	GP	G	A	TP	PIM	GP	G	A	TP	PIM
1996–97	Detroit	USHL	44	21	41	62	58	.....	.....	.....	.....	.....
1997–98	Plymouth	OHL	59	54	51	105	56	15	8	12	20	24
	United States	WJC-A	7	0	0	0	2	.....	.....	.....	.....	.....
1998–99	Plymouth	OHL	55	31	49	80	65	11	3	8	11	.....
	United States	WJC-A	6	1	3	4	.....	.....	.....	.....	.....	.....
	United States	WC-A	6	0	2	2	4	.....	.....	.....	.....	.....
	Nashville	NHL	1	0	0	0	0	.....	.....	.....	.....	.....
1999–00	Nashville	NHL	71	13	15	28	30	.....	.....	.....	.....	.....

Sergei Samsonov

YOU DON'T SEE IT OFTEN. YOU CER-tainly don't see it at your average hockey game, be it minor league or National Hockey League. But every once in a while it will appear, and when it does it will light up an arena and get the spectators to their feet.

Call it fire. Call it power. Call it extraordinarily rare—except where Sergei Samsonov is concerned.

"When you watch Sergei play, some time during the night he'll do something to make you say 'Wow!'" says Tampa Bay Lightening GM Rick Dudley, who was GM of the International Hockey League Detroit Vipers when Samsonov was a member of that team.

"He'll do something a normal player can't

do, and there are only a few players who do that every night they play."

There's no doubt that Samsonov is an exceptional player. He is, say onlookers, excitement personified, the kind of guy who will send electricity through a crowd whenever he touches the puck.

"Sergei is special," says Dudley. "I've never seen a player more dangerous when he comes out of the corner with the puck. He's almost unstoppable."

Speed, certainly, is one of the hallmarks of the twenty-two-year-old Boston left winger. Then, too, so is agility.

And strength. And poise. And power.

"Heaven help a slow-footed defenseman who has to take him one-on-one," says Bruins assistant GM Mike O'Connell. "Sergei's feet and hands look like they're going 100 miles an hour. I think the only one who knows what he's going to do is Sergei. There is a special athlete."

That assessment is pretty impressive, especially considering it's directed at a player who's a relative newcomer to the NHL. It was only three years ago, in 1997, that Samsonov became the Bruins' second pick in that year's Entry Draft.

The following season, the Moscow native was like a bullet out of the gate. He scored 22 goals and accumulated 47 points and ended up winning the Calder Trophy as best rookie in the National Hockey League.

By then, of course, he already had a few trophies on the shelf. Samsonov, who'd played two years with the Russian National Junior Team—in one season accumulating a staggering 182

points in just 50 games—was a member of the Russian team that won bronze at the World Juniors in Geneva in 1997. After graduating from junior hockey, Samsonov made a move that would clinch his entry into the NHL: he left his homeland and moved to North America to play with the IHL Detroit Vipers. It was, he says, the wisest thing he could have done.

"It was a really smart thing for me to do, coming from Russia to play in a professional league over here," he says. "Spending the year in Detroit helped me in every way . . . learning to play hockey the North American way, learning some English. The IHL is pretty much the same type of league as the NHL, it's just a different level."

To say Samsonov did well that year would be an enormous understatement. He had 64 points in 73 games, was named the IHL's Rookie of the Year, becoming the first player ever to win that award one year and the Calder the next. Samsanov, described by some observers as a Leonardo DiCaprio look-a-like, may be mighty on the ice but he isn't in stature. The 184 pound winger stands just five eight and reminds Bruins head coach Pat Burns of a "little fire hydrant." In other words, he's a compact, muscular athlete with a strong upper body and a low center of gravity.

"He's so short," says St. Louis Blues defenseman Chris Pronger, "that it's hard for a guy like me to get that far down and take him. He uses that size to his advantage."

The physical attributes are numerous, but so, too, are the mental ones. Samsanov, say those who know him, is the consummate professional, an utterly driven individual who is as good-natured as he is mature.

"Sammy is low maintenance," says coach Burns. "He works so hard in every game and every practice. He's never satisfied. I can't push him any harder than he pushes himself."

That work is paying off. In each of the three years Samsonov has been with the Bruins, he just keeps getting better. Last season, he finished with 19 goals and 26 assists for 45 points, third best on the team.

"I know what I want to do and that's just go out and play hard every game," says Samsonov. "I just want to go out and play hockey."

#14 SERGEI SAMSONOV • Boston Bruins • Left Wing

| YEAR | TEAM | LEA | REGULAR SEASON | | | | | PLAYOFFS | | | | |
			GP	G	A	TP	PIM	GP	G	A	TP	PIM
994–95	CSKA Juniors	Russia	50	110	72	182	.....	.....	.....	.....	.....	.....
	CSKA	Russia	13	2	2	4	14	.....	.....	.....	.....	.....
995–96	CSKA	Russia	51	21	17	38	12	.....	.....	.....	.....	.....
996–97	Detroit	IHL	73	29	35	64	18	.....	.....	.....	.....	.....
997–98	Boston	NHL	81	22	25	47	8	6	2	5	7	0
998–99	Boston	NHL	79	25	26	51	18	11	3	1	4	0
999–00	Boston	NHL	77	19	26	45	4	.....	.....	.....	.....	.....

#13

Patrik Stefan

IT'S A DAY PATRIK STEFAN WILL never forget.

He was eighteen. It was late June and he was at the Fleet Center in Boston with his father and grandfather. Both dad and grand-dad had been hockey players, but neither had come close to experiencing what would happen to Patrik that day.

He would be invited to play in the National Hockey League. And, incredibly, he would be No. 1 on the guest list.

"It is a perfect feeling," said Stefan's dad Karl that day. Indeed, it must have been. Not only was Patrik celebrating—so, too, were many of the residents of Pribram, the small town in the Czech Republic where Stefan was born and where he learned to play hockey.

Stefan, whom scouts had identified as a superb goal-scoring center with incredible

Of course, no hockey player—and certainly no rookie—can score two goals every game. Stefan was no exception. Even so, he did demonstrate to hockey fans that Atlanta was wise to pick him: by the end of his rookie year, he'd accumulated 5 goals and 20 assists.

Stefan, regarded by most as being remarkably mature for someone just twenty-years-old, played in the Czech Republic's elite league before coming to North America, at age seventeen, to join the International Hockey League's Long Beach Ice Dogs.

It was during his two years with the Ice Dogs that Stefan began to gather attention. He posted 17 goals and 40 assists in just 68 games with Long Beach, and in 1998 played for the Czech Republic at the World Junior Championships. Bob Butkas, a friend of Ice Dogs coach John Van Boxmeer and the man who housed Stefan while he played in California, says Stefan always had the goal of playing in the NHL in mind. "He has been totally dedicated to this moment in his life," he says.

When Butkus first met Stefan, he knew little English and felt somewhat uncomfortable in his new environment. "I knew 'work,' 'eat,' and 'sleep,'" recalls Stefan.

In time, Stefan did improve his English skills, just as he's fine-tuned his on-ice abilities. The Thrashers regard Stefan as a player with remarkable speed, passing ability and creativity on the ice. Former Thrashers winger Kelly Buchberger says Stefan also possesses a keen work ethic, something not always associated with novice hockey players.

"A lot of kids from the juniors come in and don't really appreciate what it takes over here, and that it's a privilege just to play in the league."

Not so with Stefan. He knows how far he's traveled since the day he left Pribam. He knows he's privileged to be playing on the same ice rink with the best hockey players in the world.

And, yes, as far as Atlanta coach Curt Fraser is concerned, there's no question that Stefan will continue to prove that he belongs among the best.

"Good things," he says, "are going to happen to him."

By the end of his rookie year, he'd accumulated 5 goals and 20 assists.

strength and agility, not only became the first overall pick in the 1999 NHL Entry Draft, he was also the first player to pull on an Atlanta Thrashers' uniform.

In no time, he proved he deserved it.

In Stefan's first four outings with the Thrashers, he scored five points, including two goals against his country's hockey hero.

"When I scored against Buffalo [and Dominik Hasek], it was great for me," says Stefan. "After that game, I had a couple of nice games too. But I thought, 'I hope everybody doesn't think I will always score like that.'"

#13 PATRIK STEFAN • Atlanta Thrashers • Center

			REGULAR SEASON					PLAYOFFS				
YEAR	TEAM	LEA	GP	G	A	TP	PIM	GP	G	A	TP	PIM
1997–98	Long Beach	IHL	33	11	24	35	26	10	1	1	2	2
1998–99	Long Beach	IHL	35	6	16	32	10	.....	.....	.....	.....	.....
1999–00	Atlanta	NHL	72	5	20	25	30	.....	.....	.....	.....	.....

Brad Stuart

#7

SAN JOSE SHARKS™

FUNNY HOW PEOPLE'S PATHS WILL cross.

Years ago, when a defenseman named Gary Suter first donned an NHL jersey and took to the ice for the Calgary Flames, a kid from Rocky Mountain House, Alberta, was just turning four. As the little boy grew, so did his love for hockey. He became a Flames fan, and Suter became an idol.

Today, sixteen years later, Brad Stuart has not only become a star hockey player, he also plays on the same team as his idol.

And is Suter impressed with the kid from Alberta?

Absolutely.

"He's a real natural," says Suter. "The game comes easy to him. He's so smooth, it doesn't seem like he has to work at it. It doesn't seem fair."

Fair or not, there's no questioning Stuart's talent. The rookie San Jose blueliner, who's developed a reputation as an incredibly strong and mobile player with superb hockey instincts, not only played in every game last season, he also emerged as a top candidate for the NHL's rookie award, the Calder Trophy.

"With proper training, he's going to be a Norris Trophy winner," says Suter, referring to the award which is given annually to the league's top defenseman. "The sky is the limit."

"Hey, Brad Stuart's a winner," echoes San Jose coach Darryl Sutter. "He shows up every single night, and he's impressive just because of that. . . The things

he does you want your young players to be able to do after three or four years. He does them now, and that's not something that's taught. That's God-given."

In other words, the twenty-year-old Stuart is not your average hockey player. That may be something Sharks fans have just discovered, but it's nothing new to those who've followed Stuart's career.

As a junior playing in the Western Hockey League, Stuart accumulated 67 points in a combined 59 games for the Regina Pats and the Calgary Hitmen. He helped steer the Hitmen to a league-best 51-13-8 record and the WHL championship, and was awarded the Bill Hunter Trophy as top defenseman in the league. A short time later, Stuart received two well-deserved honors: he was presented with the DeWalt

Defenseman of the Year Award and he became San Jose's No. 1 pick in the NHL Entry Draft.

"Brad Stuart is a little bit of everything," says Hitmen coach Dan Clark. Stuart, he says, is strong and aggressive and capable of playing in any game situation. "He does a little bit of everything, and he does it with a bit of a mean streak. I really enjoyed having him."

When Stuart made his entry into the NHL, he admits there were challenges he didn't face at the junior level. For one thing, there was the mental adjustment.

"If you're not ready to play, it's going to show," says Stuart, "whereas in junior you could maybe get away with it the odd night."

But Stuart says there was something else he noticed that separated the juniors from the NHL. In the big leagues, he says, everyone is watching. "I've never seen anything like it," he says. "It's close—there is a lot more meaning to every game. Every game is pretty intense. You're a little under a microscope."

It took no time for Stuart to win the notice of the NHL. Early in the season several top Shark defenseman fell victim to injury and Stuart the rookie had to carry the load.

"Traditionally, when a young guy comes along, you don't throw him into the fire as much," says coach Sutter. "Ideally, you want to ease a guy into it, especially when you make your first jaunt around the league, but, with injuries, we were forced into it."

As it turned out, Stuart not only proved he was up to the challenge, he also demonstrated that he was, quite literally, No. 1. By season's end, he'd accumulated 36 points—10 goals and 26 assists—and was the league's top-scoring rookie defenseman.

"Brad has shown, throughout his career, that he can play at a high level against the best competition his peers have to offer," says Sharks General Manager Dean Lombardi. "He plays a complete, all-round game, and if he continues to develop and work hard, he will have a bright future in the NHL."

#7 BRAD STUART • San Jose Sharks • Defense

			REGULAR SEASON					PLAYOFFS				
YEAR	TEAM	LEA	GP	G	A	TP	PIM	GP	G	A	TP	PIM
1996–97	Regina	WHL	57	7	36	43	58	.....	.....	.....	.....	.....
1997–98	Regina	WHL	72	20	45	65	82	9	3	4	7	10
1998–99	Regina	WHL	30	10	21	31	43	.....	.....	.....	.....	.....
	Calgary	WHL	29	16	20	36	58	21	8	15	23	59
	Canada	World Jr.	7	0	1	1	2	.....	.....	.....	.....	.....
1999–00	San Jose	NHL	82	10	26	36	32	12	1	0	1	6

WHEN JOE THORNTON WAS GROWING
up, he was your typical Canadian kid. He
loved hockey. He loved the NHL. And he
worshipped the ground Wayne Gretzky
walked on.

Thornton, who hails from St. Thomas,
Ontario, not far from Gretzky's old stomping
grounds of Brantford, lined the walls of his
bedroom with anything relating to The Great
One. He cheered on No. 99 when he came to
Maple Leaf Gardens. And he did something
else: he tried to copy Gretzky's every move.
It's hard to say whether the hero-worship
had anything to do with Thornton's development, but it's obvious something did. Today,
hockey watchers agree, the Boston Bruins

Former Bruins captain Ray Bourque, who's almost nineteen years Thornton's senior, says the ribbing he takes from teammates is all in fun.

"There'd be cartoons on the TV and I used to say, 'Hey, Joe, want to watch these for a while?'"

It is, of course, all a little heady for a kid from middle-class Canada who's always been known for his optimism.

"He has hardly faced any adversity in his life," says one scout. "You talk to him and he says the toughest thing he has ever had to deal with was getting cut by his peewee baseball team."

And then there was the time when Thornton was a youngster at Maple Leaf Gardens with his parents, watching a game between Toronto and Edmonton and finding himself in tears at the end of the second period. The reason? His hero—yes, Gretzky—hadn't scored yet. (Thankfully, he did in the third.)

Hockey, it seems, has always been part of Thornton's life, whether on the ice or in the middle of the road alongside big brothers John and Alex. Looking back as far as he can remember, Thornton figures he was never off the ice for more than two consecutive weeks a year, summer or winter.

Starting out, Joe did not play center but defense, since former Montreal defenseman Doug Harvey was his father's favorite player. "He wouldn't let me be a forward," Joe says of his father, Wayne, "because he didn't want me to be a cherry picker."

Thornton did not become a cherry picker (a player who cheats on defense to score goals), but he didn't become a defenseman either. He became something else: a powerful forward who would end up posting 198 points in 125 junior games with Sault Ste. Marie of the Ontario Hockey League.

In 1995–1996, he earned Rookie of the Year honors for the OHL and the Canadian Hockey League. In 1997, Thornton played at the World Junior Championships in Geneva and helped pilot the Canadians to a gold medal, something he still considers one of his best hockey memories.

It was enough to get every scout's attention.

center, who at seventeen was the No. 1 pick overall in the NHL Entry Draft, is one of the most promising young stars in the National Hockey League. No wonder. Like his idol, Thornton has speed, finesse and exceptional skills with the puck.

"He has a unique vision of the ice and is able to create and find the open spaces," says one scouting report. "[He] is a powerful shooter and an accurate passer who knows exactly when [these skills] should be used."

Yet the kid who idolized Gretzky is still very much "The Kid", in spite of the fact that he now stands six four and tips the scales at 220. At twenty-one, Thornton has barely arrived at adulthood; his Boston teammates take great pleasure in frequently reminding him of that.

"He has a unique vision of the ice and is able to create and find the open spaces."

In no time, Thornton was being hailed as something mighty special: a tough-minded, unselfish team player who tended to make things happen around the net.

In 1997 things fell into place for the kid with the Wayne Gretzky bedroom.

Boston grabbed him first overall.

"He's definitely got the game," says former Bruins defenseman Ray Bourque. "He's got the size, the speed and the skills to really be a major factor in this league and this team. I think he knows that."

Thornton's rookie season was a frustrating one as he made the difficult transition from junior hockey to the NHL. And while he struggled at times to live up to the expectations he had set for himself, as well as those set by the hockey world, he never lost his enthusiasm or his belief in himself.

That belief paid off in his sophomore season as Thornton assumed a growing role with the Bruins. He was also Boston's leading scorer with 23 goals, 37 assists in 81 games.

And so how is he enjoying life in the NHL now?

"It's not too hard at all," says the hockey player with the surfer looks and attitude. "You just go to the rink and that's what you do every day. Every day I wake up and it's like, let's go."

#6 JOE THORNTON • Boston Bruins • Center

| | | | REGULAR SEASON | | | | | PLAYOFFS | | | | |
YEAR	TEAM	LEA	GP	G	A	TP	PIM	GP	G	A	TP	PIM
1995–96	Sault Ste. Marie	OHL	66	30	46	76	51	4	1	1	2	11
1996–97	Sault Ste. Marie	OHL	59	41	81	122	123	11	11	8	19	24
1997–98	Boston	NHL	55	3	4	7	19	6	0	0	0	9
1998–99	Boston	NHL	81	16	25	41	69	11	3	6	9	4
1999–00	Boston	NHL	81	23	37	60	82	.....	.....	.....	.....	.....

Michael York

MOST KIDS, WHEN FIRST INTRODUCED to hockey, are old enough to walk. Most, when watching their first game, are old enough to focus on the ice. Not so with Michael York. Ask his family and they'll tell you that this kid visited his first hockey rink when he was just a week old. He may not have watched the game, not at first anyway, but he sure did later on. Family legend has it that he even learned to count by sitting in the stands at peewee and junior games and pointing to the numbers on the jerseys.

"It was the first sport I watched, since my brother played," says York, who hails from Waterford, Michigan, a hockey-crazed suburb of Detroit that was also home to Pat Lafontaine. "I played football, baseball and basketball; but it was my dream to play professional hockey.

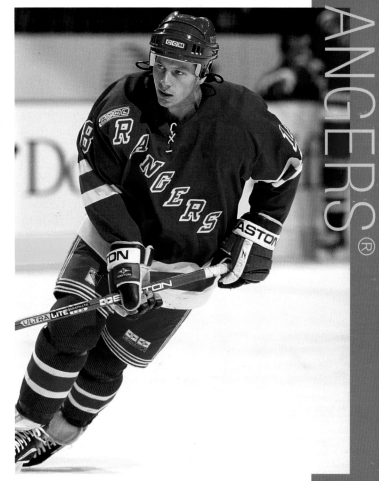

"My parents were real supportive and gave me everything I wanted hockey-wise. But they always said playing was my choice." He chose to play and play he did—exceptionally well. He worked hard at his chosen sport, and, at sixteen, went to Toronto to earn a berth in the Ontario Hockey League.

After graduating from high school, however, York changed direction. He decided he wanted to pursue a college education—and play hockey at the same time—so he enrolled at Michigan State University. The Spartans lucked out big-time.

By the time York had finished his four-year term with the Spartans, he had accumulated 79 goals and 122 assists for a whopping 201 points. He was twice a finalist for the Hobey Baker—an award given to the NCAA's best player—and was twice named an All-American. He also earned the distinction of being one of just twelve Americans to play for the U.S. National Junior Team three times.

Within just a few years, York's dream began looking as if it might come true, and in 1997 it did. That was the year he joined the National Hockey League as a member of the New York Rangers. Last season, York earned a spot on the team after demonstrating his skills at the Rangers training camp. To say that he ended up fitting into the line-up is a bit like saying that Wayne Gretzky was good on skates. The twenty-two-year-old not only impressed the crowd, he performed so well, he was named as a finalist for the Calder trophy, given annually to the league's best rookie.

"He just kept getting better and better and learning more and taking the next step every time," says John Muckler, who coached York most of last season before being relieved of his job. "Every time you thought he was going to take a step backwards, he never did. He'd have a bad game, and then he'd come out real strong the following game. When we saw that maybe two or three times, we knew he'd arrived."

York arrived all right, and he posted 50 points—26 goals and 24 assists—just to prove it. By season's end, he had shown anyone who cared to watch that he was one of the most conscientious players in hockey, a consistently dependable team player who continued to give the Rangers his all even when their fortunes were flagging.

"Mike is mature, low-key and very professional," says Rangers veteran Adam Graves, who, along with Theo Fleury, completes York's line. "He's just a good kid, level-headed. He comes to the ice rink and works every day."

It's that work ethic, that unflinching drive to succeed, that seems to make the biggest impression on people.

"Mike's a competitive guy who wants to be a good player in this league," says Fleury. "He gets his nose dirty. I tell you what: he's going to be a No. 1 center in this league for a long time. It's fun playing with him."

Like Fleury, York (or "Yorkie," as he's called by his teammates) is small by NHL standards, so he relies on his exceptional speed and vision, rather than size, to get the job done.

"I know I have to consistently prove myself every night," says York. "I just have to keep battling."

And battle he does, night after night, game after game. Today, the baby at the rink is the star of the game—not because of luck or timing, but because of old-fashioned hard work. "He's done everything he can in every game," says captain Brian Leech. "He's earned it, on his own."

#18 MICHAEL YORK • New York Rangers • Center

			REGULAR SEASON					PLAYOFFS				
EAR	TEAM	LEA	GP	G	A	TP	PIM	GP	G	A	TP	PIM
999–2000	New York Rangers	NHL	82	26	24	50	18	.....	.....	.....	.....	.....

Goalies

FOR GOALTENDER MARTIN BIRON, THE dream has always been there. It took shape when he was a grade-schooler and stayed with him as he grew.

"I dreamed about playing goal in the NHL since the first time I put on the equipment," says the netminder from Lac St. Charles, Quebec. "But that's not my only dream."

The other one is even loftier. Biron's ultimate wish has not been simply to play in the big leagues. It's been to win the Stanley Cup.

Five years ago, part of Biron's dream became reality. Regarded as a hot netminder—he'd just been named Canadian Major Junior Goaltender of the Year—Biron was recruited by the Buffalo Sabres as sixteenth overall pick in the NHL Entry Draft.

He didn't make the move immediately. Biron continued to play at the junior level for two more years and then moved on to the American League. It was there, as chief goaltender for the Rochester Americans, that Biron truly blossomed. In his first season, he set an AHL record for highest save percentage (.930), tied a thirty-one-year-old franchise record for single-season shutouts (6), and posted the AHL's lowest goals-against average in sixty years (2.07).

"He's the best goalie in the league," observed Bill Barber, coach of the AHL Philadelphia Phantoms at the time. "And he's going to play in the NHL." It was, of course, just a matter of time before Biron would make the trip to Buffalo, but even he knew that his ice time with the Sabres might be somewhat limited. After all, the organization already happened to include the man widely regarded as the most accomplished goaltender on the planet—five-time Vezina winner Dominik Hasek.

But sometimes the unpredictable happens and, in Biron's case, it did. The Sabres, who'd won the Eastern Conference banner in 1998–99, began their next season sluggishly. They started 0-5-2 and Hasek, who'd announced that summer that the season would be his last, was not his usual brilliant self. Biron got the phone call. He was recalled from Rochester and told he'd been given the start in a match-up against Carolina. The Sabres won 7-3.

A few days later Hasek suffered a groin injury and was sidelined indefinitely. Biron was immediately thrust into the No. 1 position and, before long, the Sabres' numbers began to improve.

"Marty's been very good," says Buffalo coach Lindy Ruff. "And he's great to be around. For a goalie, he almost feels human."

Anyone who's met Martin Biron would agree he's "Mr. Personality." Unlike Hasek, who tends to be somewhat quiet and solitary, Biron is animated and outgoing. He loves to talk and to laugh.

"My philosophy is always to come to practice with a smile on my face," he says. "It's not about being the funny guy, but I want to be positive and not to have my head down."

Biron, a butterfly goalie who has an exceptionally fast glove hand, has demonstrated to the

"He's great to be around. For a goalie, he almost feels human."

Sabres that, yes, life without Hasek will go on. When the Dominator does retire—he has said that will happen at the end of the 2000–2001 season—Buffalo will take comfort in knowing it has another goaltender with exceptional talent. By the end of his first season in the NHL, Biron proved he was more than capable of being No. 1, posting nineteen wins, five of them shutouts.

"Dom got in because Grant Fuhr was hurt, and that's how he became a starter in the NHL," reflects Biron. "I remember that." Biron, a tall, rather skinny netminder—he's six two and weighs only 164 pounds—remembers something else: the dream he's had since childhood.

"From the time I was about four or five, I was thinking hockey," he says. "From kindergarten, I grew up watching the Quebec Nordiques and always thought about being there."

#43 MARTIN BIRON • Buffalo Sabres • Goalie

| | | | REGULAR SEASON | | | | | | | | PLAYOFFS | | | | | |
YEAR	TEAM	LEA	GP	W	L	T	MINS	GA	SO	AVG	GP	W	L	MINS	GA	SO	AVG
1994–95	Beauport	QMJHL	56	29	16	9	3193	132	3	2.48	16	8	7	900	37	4	2.47
1995–96	Buffalo	NHL	3	0	2	0	119	10	0	5.04	....	....	....	....	....	....	....
	Beauport	QMJHL	55	29	17	7	3201	152	1	2.85	19	12	7	1134	64	0	3.39
1996–97	Beauport	QMJHL	18	6	9	1	928	61	1	3.94	....	....	....	....	....	....	....
	Hull	QMJHL	16	11	4	1	974	43	2	2.65	6	3	1	325	19	0	3.51
1997–98	Rochester	AHL	41	14	18	6	2312	113	5	2.93	4	1	3	239	16	0	4.01
	South Carolina	ECHL	2	0	1	1	86	3	0	2.09	....	....	....	....	....	....	....
1998–99	Rochester	AHL	52	36	13	3	3129	108	6	2.07	20	12	8	1167	42	1	2.16
	Buffalo	NHL	6	1	2	1	281	10	0	2.14	....	....	....	....	....	....	....
1999–00	Buffalo	NHL	41	19	18	2	2229	90	5	2.42	....	....	....	....	....	....	....

IT WILL GO DOWN AS ONE OF THE best Stanley Cup Finals ever. And it will also be remembered for some of the greatest goaltending a final series has ever seen. When it was over, only one netminder could be left standing with the Cup. And last season it was New Jersey's Martin Brodeur.

"You learn how hard it is to win the Stanley Cup," said Brodeur, moments after the Devils beat the Dallas Stars 2-1 in Game 6 of the finals. "It took us five years to get back to where we're supposed to be and now we're here. It's amazing."

The last two games of the 1999–2000 finals went into multiple overtime periods. Both games ended in the early morning hours

when most fans were asleep. And each game was highlighted by brilliants saves from Brodeur and his opponent at the other end, Eddie Belfour.

"It was the best goaltending I can remember," said Stars head coach Ken Hitchcock. "Brodeur is very difficult to beat. He was a stand-out." Maybe when you win your first Stanley Cup at the relatively tender age of twenty-three, you don't fully appreciate the moment. Maybe that's also why a much wiser, seasoned, twenty-eight-year-old Brodeur found his second Cup win especially sweet.

"I'm just so proud of all my team-mates," Brodeur said of the Devils' big win. "The second time around you understand how difficult it is to get here and the sacrifice it takes. The first time around I was too young to understand."

Brodeur's fine Stanley Cup performance capped another solid year in goal for New Jersey. In 72 games, Brodeur finished the season with a highly respectable goals against average of 2.24 and a save percentage of .910. He also became the first goalie to be credited with a game-winning goal, in his case against the Philadelphia Flyers on February 15.

As noted as he is for a lightening fast glove hand and an ability to handle the puck as well as any defensemen, Martin Brodeur has also become known as a hockey player with a child's enthusiasm for the game. Regardless of how tense the game, Brodeur always plays with a smile on his face.

"I'm just having fun," says Brodeur of the game he has played since he was a child growing up in Montreal. Brodeur also breaks another stereotype, the one that suggests that goalies are, well, a little strange; that anyone who willingly stands in front of a hard piece of rubber traveling at speeds of up to 100 mph isn't quite right in the head.

But the always affable Devils goalie has another view.

"I know some people think we're stupid," says Brodeur. "But I don't know. What about the guy who has to go get the puck when Eric Lindros is coming at him 100 mph? Who's crazier, me or him?"

"Look," he continues, "I've got a mask. I don't have any stitches. I've got my teeth. So, if one of my kids wants to be a goalie, great. I think it's a little bit safer than forward or defense."

It's safe to say that Martin Brodeur has goaltending in his blood. Literally. His father, Denis, played goal for the Canadian national team and represented his country at the 1956 Olympics where Canada finished with a bronze medal.

Young Martin also got a good look at life in the NHL, courtesy of his father's job. After his playing days were over, Denis Brodeur became the official photographer of the Montreal Canadiens. He would pay Martin five dollars to help carry his camera equipment to the arena for photo shoots and team practices.

"My dad would talk to players like Claude

Lemieux and Stephane Richer and tell them one day his son was going to play in the NHL," Brodeur remembers. "How many dads say the same thing? But, gee, he was right."

Years later, Martin Brodeur would become teammates with both Lemieux and Richer in New Jersey. It would seem Brodeur is ready to pass along his goaltending genes and experience to his own children, Anthony, four, and three-year-old twins William and Jeremy.

"We have a big rec room with two nets in it and Anthony is always wanting me to take shots on him," says Brodeur. "When I come home from practice he wants me to take shots. When he gets up from his nap, he wants shots. Along with Brodeur's wife Melanie, the entire family was front and center during last year's finals.

Often during the games, television cameras found Melanie, often in a cowboy hat, either cheering wildly or burying her face in her hands, too nervous to watch. The Brodeur children could often be seen resting their head on their mother's shoulder, their eyes barely open.

In only seven full seasons in the league, Brodeur has racked up an amazing 244 victories. If he manages to play another seven seasons and pile up wins at the same pace, Brodeur will easily smash the 400-win plateau, a milestone only a few goalies have reached. Whatever happens, we know one thing for sure. Brodeur will continue to breeze through life in

the NHL with a smile on his face.

"I tend to look at the big picture," he says. "I tend not to get overwhelmed by one performance either way."

Which seems to be a recipe for success.

#30 MARTIN BRODEUR • New Jersey Devils • Goalie

YEAR	TEAM	LEA	REGULAR SEASON								PLAYOFFS						
			GP	W	L	T	MINS	GA	SO	AVG	GP	W	L	MINS	GA	SO	AVG
1989–90	St.-Hyacinthe	QMJHL	42	23	13	2	2333	156	0	4.01	12	5	7	678	46	0	4.07
1990–91	St.-Hyacinthe	QMJHL	52	22	24	4	2946	162	2	3.30	4	0	4	232	16	0	4.14
1991–92	New Jersey	NHL	4	2	1	0	179	10	0	3.35	1	0	1	32	3	0	5.63
	St.-Hyacinthe	QMJHL	48	27	16	4	2846	161	2	3.39	5	2	3	317	14	0	2.65
1992–93	Utica	AHL	32	14	13	5	1952	131	0	4.03	4	1	3	258	18	0	4.19
1993–94	New Jersey	NHL	47	27	11	8	2625	105	3	2.40	17	8	9	1171	38	1	1.95
1994–95	New Jersey	NHL	40	19	11	6	2184	89	3	2.45	20	16	4	1222	34	3	1.67
1995–96	New Jersey	NHL	77	34	30	12	4433	173	6	2.34	....	....	....	.....	....	....	....
1996–97	New Jersey	NHL	67	37	14	13	3838	120	10	1.88	10	5	5	659	19	2	1.73
	Canada	W Cup	2	0	1	0	60	4	0	4.00	....	....	....	.....	....	....	....
1997–98	New Jersey	NHL	70	43	17	8	4128	130	10	1.89	6	2	4	366	12	0	1.97
	Canada	Olympics	DID NOT PLAY - SPARE GOALTENDER														
1998–99	New Jersey	NHL	70	39	21	10	4239	162	4	2.29	7	3	4	425	20	0	2.8
1999–00	New Jersey	NHL	72	43	20	8	4312	161	6	2.24	23	16	7	1450	39	2	1.61

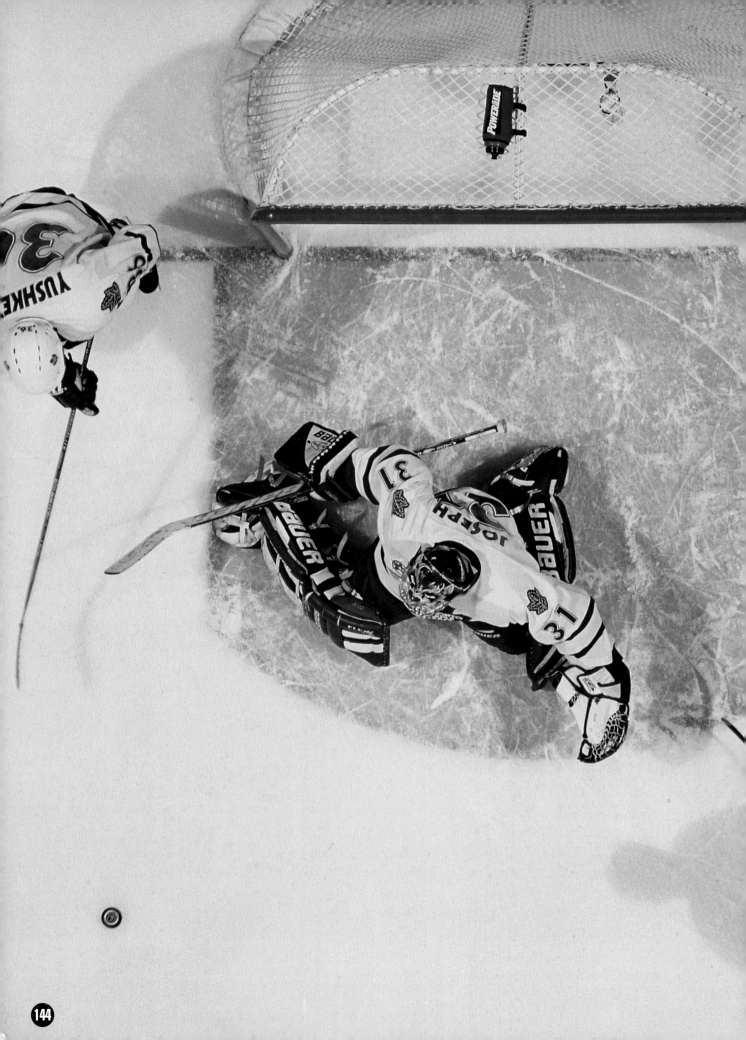

IF THERE'S ANY TRUTH TO THE
thinking that goaltenders are a bunch of
quirky, oddball eccentrics, then Toronto's
Curtis Joseph is completely out of the norm.

Joseph has none of the stereotypical peculi-
arities often associated with those hockey
players who willingly have missiles shot at
them from point-blank range. He is, in fact,
your average suburban father of three—
except, of course, that he's also one of the premier goalies in the National Hockey League,
good enough that last season he was a Vezina
finalist for the second consecutive year.

Joseph's boyhood friend Martin Harding,
says his pal is a salt-of-the-earth kind of guy,
a soft-spoken, modest man whose favorite
moments are spent at home with his wife,
his kids and his horses.

"A reporter from Edmonton once called me asking for dirt on Curtis and I just laughed," says Harding. "His only weakness may be his indecisiveness. After a game, he took forever to decide between KFC and pizza."

The thirty-three-year-old Joseph, who last season helped lead the Toronto Maple Leafs out of the regular season and into the playoffs, began his hockey season at the age of eleven—and only because of happenstance.

"[I] had a cousin who was playing in King City (north of Toronto) who was moving, and his mother had paid the fee. I kind of took his spot. He was a goalie and I couldn't skate, so I went in net and fell down a lot, and everyone told me I was pretty good at it. I just stuck with it and, eventually, I could skate."

He could also do something else: stop the puck. Joseph, say observers, was a natural even then. He may have had a style that defied description—in many ways, he still does—but there was no questioning his speed, his agility and his determination to keep his net puck-free.

Joseph, who's better known in hockey circles as Cujo, had an unorthodox childhood, to put it mildly. His now legendary story begins in Keswick, Ontario, where he was born to an unwed seventeen-year-old. As a toddler, he was

> "His only weakness may be his indecisiveness. After a game, he took forever to decide between Kentucky Fried Chicken and pizza."

adopted by a middle-aged hospital nurse who raised him in a special care home, where she and her husband tended to men with brain injuries.

"It's sad to say he didn't have a great family life growing up, so now he and his wife and kids cherish their time together," says Harding. "I think that's why he's so devoted to his kids."

Joseph spent his grade school years in Sharon, Ontario, and then moved to Newmarket for high school, where he played football, fastball, basketball, and ball hockey.

"He was as good, if not better, playing out than he was in net," recalls Harding of his pal's stint on the high school ball hockey team.

At the age of twenty, when Joseph was seemingly beyond draft age, he moved to Saskatchewan, where he attended Notre Dame College. Again, it was happenstance—or fate—that changed the course of his life.

Rod Brind'Amour also happened to be playing for the Notre Dame Hounds, and college scouts were packing into the arena to get a look at him. They did, but they also got a look at someone else: the goalie with the lightning-quick glove hand.

Joseph ended up steering the Hounds to the national championship that year, and in no time he was receiving invitations from American colleges. He settled on the University of Wisconsin, but remained there for only a year before signing, in 1989, with the St. Louis Blues.

In 1995, he moved north again and spent three years deflecting pucks for the Edmonton Oilers. It was there that he truly attained stardom, and where he endeared himself to fans.

"There have been three icons in this city," Bill Tuele, a representative with the Oilers media relations department, once said. "Wayne Gretzky, Dave Semenko and Curtis Joseph. Curtis obviously didn't have the attention Wayne did, but in terms of impact on this city he was every bit Wayne's equal. I hate to use the word, but he's just a nice man."

By July 1998, Joseph was on the move again, this time back to the province where he was born. Joseph, who's taken up residence north of Toronto, says the move to the Maple

Leafs was definitely a homecoming of sorts.

"Growing up north of Toronto, I idolized most of the players who played on the Maple Leafs," he says. "To actually put the sweater on and be part of the Maple Leaf team is extremely exciting."

It's exciting, too, for the fans in Toronto, who've watched their team become re-energized with Joseph in the net. In each of the two seasons Joseph has been with the Leafs, the team has been a playoff contender, advancing to the third round in 1998–99 and to the second last year.

But in spite of all that—and in spite of the fact that he posted a save percentage of .915 last season and was acknowledged as one of the best goaltenders in the National Hockey league—Curtis Joseph is one hockey player who has his priorities in check. He loves his hockey, but there's something he loves more.

"At the rink, there's all this attention, and that's nice," he says. "But I enjoy being home. I can just be dad, the guy who takes the garbage out."

#31 CURTIS JOSEPH • Toronto Maple Leafs • Goalie

YEAR	TEAM	LEA	GP	W	L	T	MINS	GA	SO	AVG	GP	W	L	MINS	GA	SO	AVG
						REGULAR SEASON							PLAYOFFS			
1988–89	Univ. Wisconsin	WCHA	38	21	11	5	2267	94	1	2.49	....	....	....	....	....	....	....
1989–90	St. Louis	NHL	15	9	5	1	852	48	0	3.38	6	4	1	327	18	0	3.30
	Peoria Rivermen	IHL	23	10	8	2	1241	80	0	3.87	....	....	....	....	....	....	....
1990–91	St. Louis	NHL	30	16	10	2	1710	89	0	3.12	....	....	....	....	....	....	....
1991–92	St. Louis	NHL	60	27	20	10	3494	175	2	3.01	6	2	4	379	23	0	3.64
1992–93	St. Louis	NHL	68	29	28	9	3890	196	1	3.02	11	7	4	715	27	2	2.27
1993–94	St. Louis	NHL	71	36	23	11	4127	213	1	3.10	4	0	4	246	15	0	3.66
1994–95	St. Louis	NHL	36	20	10	1	1914	89	1	2.79	7	3	3	392	24	0	3.67
1995–96	Las Vegas	IHL	15	12	2	1	874	29	1	1.99	....	....	....	....	....	....	....
	Edmonton	NHL	34	15	16	2	1936	111	0	3.44	....	....	....	....	....	....	....
	Canada	WC-A	8	....	....	....	409	12	....	1.94	....	....	....	....	....	....	....
1996–97	Canada	W Cup	7	5	2	0	468	18	1	2.00	....	....	....	....	....	....	....
	Edmonton	NHL	72	32	29	9	4100	200	6	2.93	12	5	7	767	36	2	2.82
1997–98	Edmonton	NHL	71	29	31	9	4132	181	8	2.63	12	5	7	716	23	3	1.93
	Canada	Olympics					DID NOT PLAY - SPARE GOALTENDER										
1998–99	Toronto	NHL	67	35	24	7	4001	171	3	2.56	17	9	8	1011	41	1	2.43
1999–00	Toronto	NHL	63	36	20	7	3801	158	4	2.49	12	6	6	729	25	1	2.06

Steve Shields

MOST DISTINGUISHED GOALTENDERS are noted for things like shutouts and save percentages. Some, like San Jose's Steve Shields, are also standouts because of something else—their personality. Shields, say those who know him, is not only a red-hot goalie, he's a really nice guy.

"Steve is an easy-going guy, a wonderful young man," says legendary goalie coach Mitch Korn, who coached Shields when he backed up Dominik Hasek in Buffalo. "I don't think he has a selfish bone in his body."

He may be good-natured and unselfish, but he's also one of the toughest, most determined players in the National Hockey League.

"He really impresses me with his work ethic and desire," says fellow Shark Vincent Damphousse. "That's why I think he's going to be a good goaltender for a long time."

The prediction is undoubtedly a safe one. If Shields continues to perform like he did last season, he will remain an exceptional goalie for a long time to come.

It was this year that the twenty-eight-year-old Shields finally got his first serious opportunity to be an NHL starter—and he proved that he was up to the task. He posted a regular

season save percentage of .911, recorded four shutouts, and piloted the Sharks into the play-offs. He played a key role in the Sharks' first-round playoff series upset over the heavily favored St. Louis Blues.

"Shields is a huge part of the success of the San Jose Sharks," observes Nashville Predators coach Barry Trotz, who considers Shields one of the premier goal-tenders in the league.

"They have a very talented team, but we played them twice early in the season and should have won both games: we outshot them both times. In one game, we had fifty-two shots on him and they won the game 5-1. Shields was the difference."

Shields, a Toronto native who grew up idolizing netminder Ken Dryden, established himself as an outstanding goalie long before he entered the NHL. He played for the University of Michigan for four years and was twice named an All-American.

In 1991, he was drafted by the Buffalo Sabres. He didn't head to the big leagues immediately but went instead to Rochester of the American League, something he now feels was extremely beneficial in terms of confidence-building.

"I think it does everybody good to spend time in the minors, because you learn how to play an important role on a professional team," he says. "You know you can hide a forward on a team in the NHL, but if you're in the minors, you're going to be put in key situations because you're there to learn, you're there to develop."

Eventually, when Shields got his chance to stand between the pipes in Buffalo, he found himself playing behind the man widely considered to be the best in the world. Consequently, Shields spent more time watching Dominik Hasek than tending goal.

In three seasons with the Sabres, Shields appeared in only thirty-one games. He learned to be patient. He also learned how to tend goal by watching Hasek's every move. Shields may have developed his own personal style, but some of his moves—like his habit of dropping

his stick to cover the puck—are pure Hasek. Shields' tenure in Buffalo was in many ways like attending goalie school, but by June 1998, when he was traded to San Jose, he was more than ready for graduation. He garnered more playing time in California, splitting his duties with Mike Vernon until Vernon was sidelined with a second-half injury.

Shields, who at six three and 215 pounds is one of the biggest goalies in the league, was instantly propelled into the No. 1 spot and took no time winning rave reviews. He embarked on a career-best eleven-game unbeaten streak and set a team record save percentage of .921.

Several months later, toward the end of December, Vernon was traded to Florida. For the first time in his NHL career, Shields was second to no one. His coach, not one to mince words, was extremely pleased with his goalie's performance.

"Steve Shields has been unbelievable for us," said Darryl Sutter a few months after Shields took on the No. 1 job. Shields' teammates have been equally impressed and describe their netminder as their anchor on the ice.

"[Shields' play] gives the whole team confidence," says rookie Brad Stuart. "When you see your goalie making big saves for you, it takes a little pressure off."

Winger Jeff Friesen agrees and admits that there were nights last season when the Sharks emerged the victor only because of their goalie. "I don't know what to say about him," he says. "He's the real deal. He's a great goaltender."

#31 STEVE SHIELDS • San Jose Sharks • Goalie

			REGULAR SEASON							PLAYOFFS						
YEAR	TEAM	LEA	GP	W	L	T	MINS	GA	SO	AVG	GP	W	L	MINS	GA	SO	AVG
1990–91	Uni of Mich.	CCHA	37	26	6	3	1963	106	0	3.24	....	....	....	....	....	....	....
1991–92	Uni of Mich.	CCHA	37	27	7	2	2090	99	1	2.84	....	....	....	....	....	....	....
1992–93	Uni of Mich.	CCHA	39	30	6	2	2027	75	2	2.22	....	....	....	....	....	....	....
1993–94	Uni of Mich.	CCHA	36	28	6	1	1961	87	0	2.66	....	....	....	....	....	....	....
1994–95	Rochester	AHL	13	3	8	0	673	53	0	4.72	1	0	0	20	3	0	9.00
	South Carolina	ECHL	21	11	5	2	1158	52	2	2.69	3	0	2	144	11	0	4.58
1995–96	Buffalo	NHL	2	1	0	0	75	4	0	3.20	....	....	....	....	....	....	....
	Rochester	AHL	43	20	17	2	2357	140	1	3.56	19	15	3	1127	47	1	2.50
1996–97	Buffalo	NHL	13	3	8	2	789	39	0	2.97	10	4	6	570	26	1	2.74
	Rochester	AHL	23	14	6	2	1331	60	1	2.70	....	....	....	....	....	....	....
1997–98	Buffalo	NHL	16	3	6	4	785	37	0	2.83	....	....	....	....	....	....	....
	Rochester	AHL	1	0	1	0	59	3	0	3.04	....	....	....	....	....	....	....
1998–99	San Jose	NHL	37	15	11	8	2162	80	4	2.22	1	0	1	60	6	0	6.00
1999–00	San Jose	NHL	67	27	30	8	3797	162	4	2.56	12	5	7	696	36	0	3.10

Roman Turek

THE STORY IS A FAMILIAR ONE. Young boy wants to play hockey, comes to first practice, and is handed a pair of goalie pads—not because he's asked for them but because no one else wants to put them on. Roman Turek knows the story well. After all, he's appeared in it. He was seven years old, the son of dairy workers, a little boy who hailed from the town of Strakonice in the Czech Republic. Back then, on that fateful day when young Turek arrived at his first hockey practice, he found himself at the end of a long line of little boys.

The coaches were handing out equipment. When Turek finally had his turn, he was given all that was left: goalie gear. But he didn't complain. In fact, he found he rather enjoyed playing anchor for his team.

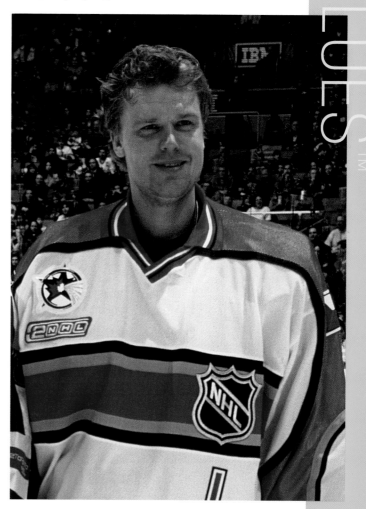

That's not to say, however, that he didn't assemble an impressive record prior to last season.

Turek played five junior seasons with Budejovice in the Czech League and in one—1993–1994—was named MVP. He has performed many times on the world stage, representing the Czech Republic at the World Championships in 1993 and 1994.

In 1996 he was back at the Worlds, where he led the Czechs to a gold medal, posting a 7-0-1 record in eight games.

In 1990, he was named Minnesota's sixth choice in the NHL entry draft. Life, for Roman Turek, would never be quite the same. When he arrived in North America, he entered a foreign world. He found the hockey different—the rinks were smaller than the ones he was used to and there seemed to be more traffic in front of the net. There were also language barriers facing Turek, his wife Helena, and their young son Eddie. "When we came to the States, I didn't speak any English," he says. "At first I could just say 'Hi' and 'Bye.'"

He did learn the language, thanks to the television set and his teammates. And he also learned a lot more about his game. He spent parts of two seasons goaltending in Kalamazoo, Michigan, before getting the call from the Dallas Stars.

It was in 1996–1997 that Turek made his NHL debut, going 3-1 and recording a GAA of 2.05. Two years later, the year the Stars became Stanley Cup champions, he finished at 16-3-3 with a GAA of 2.02.

Still, he wasn't No. 1 in Dallas, Turek was playing second fiddle to Eddie Belfour and that simply wasn't good enough. Like his fellow countryman, goaltender Dominik Hasek, Turek had a dream when he left his homeland for the United States: to be backup to no one. "I came here to be a first goalie," he says. "First, I played for the farm team in Michigan. Then, I was happy when I stayed in Dallas. Now, I want to play first goalie."

For Turek, that opportunity arrived in June 1999, when he was acquired by St. Louis in exchange for a third-round draft choice in the

"Really, I felt comfortable there rather quickly," he recalls. And, yes, he is comfortable still.

Roman Turek has, of course, traveled light years since the days of starter hockey.

Today, he is thirty, a six three, 215 pound goalie whose nickname, not surprisingly, is "Large."

He is also something else: one of the most valued members of the St. Louis Blues.

"He's the most important guy on our team," says Blue winger Pavol Demitra. "He's why we have so many points. He's playing unbelievable."

You simply can't argue with the stats. By season's end, he had recorded 42 wins and had a GAA of 1.95—second only to Philadelphia's Brian Boucher. Not bad, especially considering it was just Turek's first year as a No. 1 goaltender in the NHL.

"He is," says Demitra, "the top goalie in the league right now."

1999 entry draft. Within a couple of months, St. Louis traded netminder Grant Fuhr to Calgary and the No. 1 job went to Turek.

Turek, of course, is thrilled with the way things turned out and so are his teammates.

They saw immediately what Turek had to offer: a solid team player who maintains an almost unbelievable level of calm, no matter how stressful the situation. "He is," says Demitra, "the top goalie in the league right now."

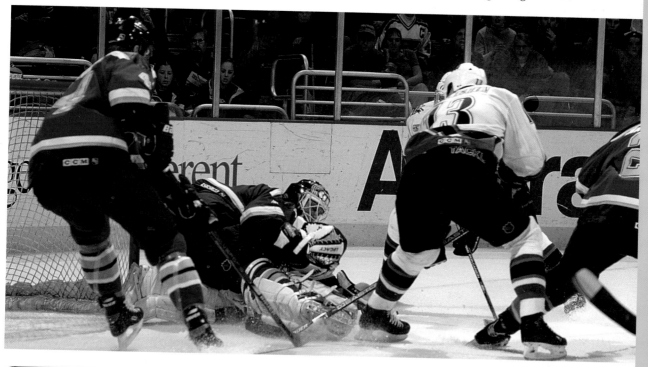

#1 ROMAN TUREK • St. Louis Blues • Goalie

| YEAR | TEAM | LEA | REGULAR SEASON | | | | | | | | PLAYOFFS | | | | | | |
			GP	W	L	T	MINS	GA	SO	AVG	GP	W	L	MINS	GA	SO	AVG
1987–88	Czechoslovakia	EJC-A	5	0	0	0	273	9	0	1.98	....	....	....	....	....	....	....
1988–89	Czechoslovakia	WJC-A	7	0	0	0	390	16	0	2.46	....	....	....	....	....	....	....
1989–90	Czechoslovakia	WJC-A	6	0	0	0	326	14	0	2.57	....	....	....	....	....	....	....
1990–91	Budejovice	Czech.	26	0	0	0	1244	98	0	4.70	....	....	....	....	....	....	....
1991–92	Budejovice	Czech-2							DID NOT PLAY								
1992–93	Budejovice	Czech	43	0	0	0	2555	121	0	2.84	....	....	....	....	....	....	....
	Czech Republic	WC-A							DID NOT PLAY								
1993–94	Budejovice	Cze-Rept	4	0	0	0	2584	111	0	2.51	3	0	0	180	12	0	4.0
	Czech Republic	Olympics	20	0	0	120	3	0	1.50	....	....	....	....	....	....	....	....
	Czech Republic	WC-A	2	0	0	0	120	4	0	2.00	....	....	....	....	....	....	....
1994–95	Budejovice	Cze-Rept	4	0	0	0	2587	119	0	2.76	9	0	0	498	25	0	3.0
	Czech Republic	WC-A	6	3	3	0	359	9	0	1.50	....	....	....	....	....	....	....
1995–96	Nurnberg	Germany	8	0	0	0	2787	154	0	3.31	5	0	0	338	14	0	2.4
	Czech Republic	WC-A	8	7	0	1	480	15	0	1.88	....	....	....	....	....	....	....
1996–97	Czech Republic	W Cup	3	0	3	0	82	10	0	7.00	....	....	....	....	....	....	....
	Dallas	NHL	6	3	1	0	263	9	0	2.05	....	....	....	....	....	....	....
	Michigan	IHL	29	8	13	4	1555	77	0	2.97	....	....	....	....	....	....	....
1997–98	Dallas	NHL	23	11	10	1	1324	49	1	2.22	....	....	....	....	....	....	....
	Michigan	IHL	2	1	1	0	119	5	0	2.51	....	....	....	....	....	....	....
1998–99	Dallas	NHL	26	16	3	3	1382	48	1	2.08	....	....	....	....	....	....	....
1999–00	St. Louis	NHL	67	42	15	9	3960	129	7	1.95	7	3	4	415	19	0	2.75

DANIEL AND HENRIK SEDIN
forwards
VANCOUVER CANUCKS
Next year will be their highly-anticipated debut.

PAVEL BRENDL
forward
NEW YORK RANGERS
Next year will be his highly-anticipated debut.

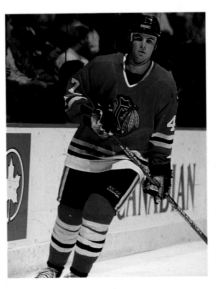

SIMON GAGNE
forward
PHILADELPHIA FLYERS
Great rookie season. Played great in the playoffs. Could be a star in the making.

STEVE McCARTHY
defense
CHICAGO BLACK HAWKS
Saw limited action as a rookie. Played junior mostly, but everyone agrees he will be great.

ROBYN REGEHR
defense
CALGARY FLAMES
Great rookie season. Will be a star.

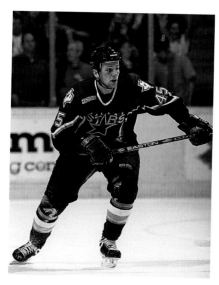

BRENDAN MORROW
forward
DALLAS STARS
Played with Mike Modano.
Will be a leader of the future
on this team.

BRIAN FINLEY
goalie
NASHVILLE PREDATORS
A No. 5 draft pick that great
things are expected of.

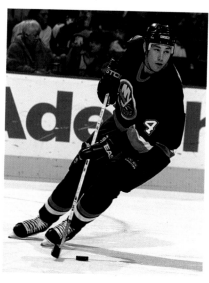

ERIC BREWER
defense
EDMONTON OILERS
Will see his full force when
he plays more next season.
A true up-and-comer.

ALEX TANGUAY
forward
COLORADO AVALANCHE
Great player who had fine rookie
season. Is almost overlooked
because the Avs have so many
great young players like Chris
Drury and Milan Hejduk.

MAXIME OUELLET
goalie
PHILADELPHIA FLYERS
Starred for Canada at World
Juniors. He and Brian Boucher
should give the Flyers some of
the strongest goaltending in the
league and they're both young.

PHOTO CREDITS

All photographs were provided by NHL Images

Barry Gossage — 50, 59, 67, 153

Craig Melvin — 4, 10, 12, 13, 15, 18, 19, 20, 24, 35, 44, 45, 46, 49, 61, 70, 71, 72, 74, 77, 81, 86, 87, 90, 91, 94, 95, 97, 99, 102, 105, 107, 109, 114, 122, 123, 125, 126, 128, 132, 134, 135, 158, 159

Dave Sandford — 5, 8, 9, 11, 16, 21, 26, 34, 43, 47, 52, 54, 58, 60, 62, 63, 64, 73, 75, 76, 78, 80, 96, 106, 110, 112, 117, 120, 129, 138, 139, 142, 144, 145, 146, 147, 148, 154, 156, 158

Diane Sobolewski — 17, 27, 32, 51, 57, 79, 88, 89, 113, 124, 133, 158

Don Smith — 55, 119, 121, 152

Gregg Forwerck — 23, 25, 104, 115, 116, 158, 159

Jeff Vinnick — 33, 37, 39, 158, 159

Joe Patronite — 22

Joel Quenneville — 155

Kent Smith — 14, 42, 100, 101, 111, 127

Mitchell Layton — 41, 53, 65, 108, 140, 141, 157

Nevin Reid — 28, 30, 31, 36, 38, 40, 48, 56, 82, 83, 84, 93, 118, 150, 151

Ray Grabowski — 29, 103

Tim De Frisco — 85, 92, 98

ACKNOWLEDGEMENTS

Many of the quotes contained in this book first appeared in newspapers, magazines, and in-house publications of NHL teams throughout the United States and Canada. The authors would like to acknowledge the following:

The St. Louis Post-Dispatch
Sports Illustrated
The Rocky Mountain News
The Denver Post
The Boston Globe
Powerplay Magazine
The Hockey News
The Boston Herald
The Buffalo News
Sports Spectrum
Canadian Hockey Magazine
The Orange County Register
The L.A. Times
The Atlanta Journal-Constitution
The Calgary Sun
The Tennessean
The Flint Journal
Hockeytown Magazine
ESPN The Magazine
The Tampa Bay Times
The Tampa Bay Tribune
San Jose Sharks Magazine
The San Francisco Chronicle
The C.C. Times
The Edmonton Sun
The San Jose Mercury News
The Ottawa Sun
The Ottawa Citizen
Inthecrease.com
Game Night
The New York Daily News
The New York Times
Top Shelf
The Santa Rosa Press Democrat
Harnett's Sports Arizona
The Sun Sentinel
The Miami Herald
The Sporting News
The Star Ledger
The Record
The New York Post
USA Today
Hockey Digest

The authors also wish to thank The Media Relations Department of the National Hockey League teams whose players are profiled in this book.